Minimalism and Decluttering

How to Clear Your Clutter and
Enjoy the Benefits of a Tidy Home

*(Tricks & Tips to Live Better With Less as a
Minimalist and Embracing Happiness)*

Dave H Culligan

Published By **Regina Loviusher**

Dave H Culligan

All Rights Reserved

Minimalism and Decluttering: How to Clear Your Clutter and Enjoy the Benefits of a Tidy Home (Tricks & Tips to Live Better With Less as a Minimalist and Embracing Happiness)

ISBN 978-1-77485-959-9

No part of this guidebook shall be reproduced in any form without permission in writing from the publisher except in the case of brief quotations embodied in critical articles or reviews.

Legal & Disclaimer

The information contained in this ebook is not designed to replace or take the place of any form of medicine or professional medical advice. The information in this ebook has been provided for educational & entertainment purposes only.

The information contained in this book has been compiled from sources deemed reliable, and it is accurate to the best of the Author's knowledge; however, the Author cannot guarantee its accuracy and validity and cannot be held liable for any errors or omissions. Changes are periodically made to this book. You must consult your doctor or get professional medical advice before using any of the suggested remedies, techniques, or information in this book.

Upon using the information contained in this book, you agree to hold harmless the Author from and against any damages, costs, and expenses, including any legal fees potentially resulting from the application of any of the information provided by this guide. This disclaimer applies to any damages or injury caused by the use and application, whether directly or indirectly, of any advice or information presented, whether for breach of contract, tort, negligence, personal injury, criminal intent, or under any other cause of action.

You agree to accept all risks of using the information presented inside this book. You need to consult a professional medical practitioner in order to ensure you are both able and healthy enough to participate in this program.

Table Of Contents

Introduction 1

Chapter 1: Do We Really Need All This Stuff? 4

Chapter 2: Why A Minimalist Home? 11

Chapter 3: Lifestyle Habits For Minimalist Living 19

Chapter 4: Minimalist Home Decor 27

Chapter 5: Cleaning The Clutter - Donating Is Caring 37

Chapter 6: How To Declutter Your Home 50

Chapter 7: Simple Ways To Stay Healthy For Decades 57

Chapter 8: Decluttering In Your Home ... 71

Chapter 9: Arranging And Decluttering Outdoors/Porch 85

Chapter 10: The Benefits Of A Simple Life 95

Chapter 11: Declutter And Promote Happiness 102

Chapter 12: How You Can Overcome Your Digital Addiction 115

Chapter 13: Making Minimalistic Decisions And The Benefits It Offer 141

Chapter 14: How To Make Digital Minimalism Your Way In Life 153

Chapter 15: How Do You Organize Your Bathroom? 162

Chapter 16: Applying Minimalism To Meditation 172

Conclusion 183

Introduction

What images spring to your mind when the word "minimalism" is mentioned? Imagine living with 100 things in your house. Do you want to live in a home that doesn't have a TV, a car, or furniture? Living in less desirable areas around the world is not an option. Not having children, no matter how much you want them.

This is why minimalism is so appealing to most people. Some people consider minimalism a fad. Others are quick to say that they would never become minimalist because of the many restrictions mentioned above.

The good news about minimalism is that it has absolutely nothing to do whatever I have mentioned, as well as any other misinformation. In reality, minimalism can help people achieve their goals and enjoy the best things in life. While minimalism may be helpful if you are looking to have fewer possessions, that is not the main point.

So what is minimalism exactly? What are the benefits of becoming a minimalist?

Minimalism covers many aspects of daily life - time, money, homes and more - but this book focuses only on the minimalist home.

Do you value freedom and no worry? Do you desire to live a life of freedom from anxiety, guilt, and depression? No matter where you are, there's one thing common: We have developed a strong consumer culture in many cities around the globe. Are you seeking a way out from the consumer culture most of us have built our lives on?

Is your home so uncomfortable that it causes you to be anxious when you get home? Are you seeking peace, freedom and beauty for your home?

If the answer to any of these questions is YES then you should read this book. The remaining pages will reveal what you can expect when you finish the book.

Understanding that less can be more

Benefits of a minimalist home

Tips for making your decluttering exercise fun

Let go of your negative mindset and learn new ways to live clutter-free.

Find creative ways to organize your home.

Live free from the burdens of material possessions while achieving true peace within your home

This book will show you how to get rid of the burdens of your past. You'll learn how to create peace and harmony in your life, as well as freedom from guilt, despair, overwhelm, and stress from material possessions. Are you ready get rid clutter and be clutter free? Let's begin!

Chapter 1: Do We Really Need All This Stuff?

Shelter, food, and clothing are all essential human needs. After these three basic human needs are met, there is no need for us to have any other means of survival. In my 40 year-old life, I experienced both excess and scarcity. My life experiences have led me to believe that minimalism gives us the best chance to live our lives with intention. Growing up poor led to me accumulating material later in my life. It was my childhood that left me with a deep impression. I was the oldest among three daughters. Even though my parents were both employed, our family was barely surviving paycheck to paycheck. There was never enough money to cover even the most basic needs. I'll never forget the billowing curtains hidden behind closed windows. Through tiny cracks, wind always found its way in the room. The good news is that the apartment has never seen mold. The constant air movement must have played an important role in this.

In winter, our house was rarely heated. There were two options for the long frigid nights. There were only two options during the long frigid nights. One was to lay down beneath the many layers of heavy bed cover with one's head under, with oxygen barely reaching the lungs and feeling the threatening threat of suffocation. Keep your face high and the cold airstream inhaled will give you a sore throat for several days. Switching between them at regular intervals was a way to keep me busy until dawn.

Our shoes, and clothing, mostly handcrafted and second-hand were worn until they began to fall apart or become too small.

When I was fourteen, the soles of my shoes were split and I went to school in snow. My father attached the separate sole parts of my shoes with three pieces copper wire each. My mother gave me plastic bags and tied them around my ankles. This was to protect my feet from the snow and slush. As I sat in class, I had my feet constantly under the table and reminded myself not to slip on my soles to prevent others from seeing my footwear. There were only two weeks to go before my next paycheck.

We never tossed food out, as no edibles were left behind long enough for spoilage.

My childhood, and my early adolescence, were filled with horrible experiences. The majority of them ran the gamut of dark colors. At sixteen, my suspicions about the existence of a mysterious and benevolent force in this universe began to grow. It was at that time I fell in love and married my husband three years later. We moved in with each other, went to the same college, and I don't believe there is anyone in the world happier than us. We started with what we could fit in our luggages and saved the rest. Each year brought us a little more money. The turning point was when we decided to jump on the consumerism train. We began to browse the internet and to buy things. It was very enjoyable and fun. I was happy to see the end of my years of being poor. I saw each acquisition as a badge of ability to provide a better standard of living. Over the past twenty years, we've moved nine more times. We have lived in various cities, and even different countries. It was very simple in the beginning. You just need to pack a few boxes before you go. Things became more complicated with each subsequent move.

We had planned to move on one of these days months in advance. We have been planning our moves by packing what we want and disposing off the rest. But, due to insufficient space in our moving truck, we ended up with seven large boxes of material possessions, as well as several furniture pieces, on the street.

A decade ago, we stopped inviting other family members over due to the unsightliness in our living spaces. There was so much stuff, you couldn't find a place on the ground to put your feet. Apart from the overflowing cabinets and closets, there was also a lot of stuff. We installed shelves from floor up in all rooms, including the bathroom, kitchen, hallway, basement and hall. This allowed us to store more stuff vertically as well as horizontally. Many storage containers with diverse items were found on top of kitchen cabinets, wardrobes, and under the beds. Numerous binders, boxes of miscellaneous things, magazines stacked up, CDs/DVDs, appliances for every purpose, skin and haircare products, various tools. The search for a document took us 2 days. Although I did manage to find the document, I kept a mental record of it so I could remember where it was. It took us three more hours to find it again when we needed it. Many times we purchased an item just because we needed it immediately, even though it was likely that there was another item with the exact same functionality hidden amongst all the clutter. It was faster and more convenient to buy a replacement than to go through the mess to find the original one.

A few years back, the basement of our apartment block was robbed. The thief got away a few days later. He had been looking through the stuff of our neighbor and mine. Our neighbor was missing an older toy train collection. However, we weren't able to tell the police exactly what was missing from our possessions. Perhaps he was overwhelmed with the clutter, which was well-organized in boxes and shelves, when he opened his door. Perhaps he may have taken some things but we haven't noticed them disappearing. We won't ever know.

Decluttering was something we decided to do out of necessity, as the apartment was in danger of burst. We were ready to let go of our most treasured possessions. It was very painful. The majority of the items are brand new and never worn. They were expensive, so I decided to make a profit by selling them. These were almost all new or lightly-used, high-quality items. It took us so many hours to take pictures and create and track listings. We also had to communicate with potential buyers. Finally, we went to the postoffice to ship the goods. All of it went out for less than half the original cost. It took us a while to get there. After a few months, we began donating and giving away stuff. This was faster but it didn't make any money. The satisfaction of knowing our stuff would be useful and appreciated was enough to keep us going.

We got a glimpse at some of our floor spaces. All those mountains of stuff that we were getting out the doors used to amount to money. Every item was putting a strain on our planet. It was difficult to comprehend how people could be so reckless and negligent for so many years.

Chapter 2: Why A Minimalist Home?

There are many TV programs that feature makeovers. Many of us would love to be part of such shows. People who are unhappy about their homes get the chance to have it transformed on the home makeover show. The design experts would evaluate the

property and provide suggestions to improve it.

The renovation team would then be sent to do the repairs and upgrades as well as furnish new furniture and decorations. Finally, the team will be invited for the "big reveal", where they often get excited about the new look. The house could look better with new furnishings, decorations, and electronic devices.

However, one question immediately springs to mind: after all the excitement over the decoration, does their new home really make any difference in the lives of their family? The renovation will cost them more in time, money, and energy to maintain than their original home. Are their new surroundings more important to them than their previous home?

It's a fact that not all of us are chosen to feature on home makeover TV shows. Many people are disappointed by the state of their living rooms. Many of us have spent so much on buying items for our homes. We spent a lot time organizing, cleaning, and maintaining all of the stuff we bought.

It ends up looking like a place we won't live in, even when we have some time to enjoy it after work or on weekends. It is now time to ask the big question: What can you do?

Some people, who are not afraid to give up, go further and look for answers elsewhere. This includes browsing online, watching TV commercials, and visiting showrooms. Finally, they decide that buying more or better stuff is the best solution.

Some people don't get the fundamental satisfaction they seek, even when they do make an effort to improve their home. Are you able to see the true problem? Did you ever wonder if the solution is buying more household items, having enough properties, or managing the ones that are already there?

Are you happy in the home that you have? Is it the home that you want to live in? What if instead of living in the homes we desire, we are being pushed to buy the homes we think we should have. It is essential that we make minimal changes to our homes if we want happiness and contentment in our lives.

Now, think about it. Are you open to exploring something other than the usual stuff? Are you open to looking inwards, rather than outside? Are you willing to work with others to create a home that represents you and your values?

Do you ever look forward to coming home every day? You will find more joy owning less property than owning all of the expensive properties. Based on many years of experience I can tell you that getting rid off the clutter in your house will make your life easier.

A Minimalist House is a Good Idea

You can reap many benefits from living a minimalist life. If we get rid of most of the stuff that we don't actually need, we can enjoy a minimalist lifestyle. It is possible to realize how little we really need to survive when you really stop and think.

It's not necessary to surround yourself with all the stuff. It is important to remember that "less is more." Living with fewer possessions will bring you these benefits:

You can make space for the most important things

Yes, it is possible to create space in your rooms, closets, drawers, kitchen, and other areas by clearing out your clutter. This allows your body to breathe and gives you the space to fill up your life instead with unnecessary items.

You gain more freedom

Did you realize that the stuff we keep at home can act as an anchor, tying us down.

Are you afraid of losing the things you have at your home? It's normal to be afraid of losing all the things we own. Fear of losing all of our stuff is something we often fear. However, you will find a sense of liberation like you have never experienced before when you let go of your stuff - freedom from overworking, debt, and obsession.

A minimalist home is a place you feel more at home and where you have more to look forward too

If your home is clutter-free, you will find it more relaxing and less stressful. This is because you will have less things to focus on. You will find yourself valuing your home more, and making the best use of what little you do have. It's now possible to put more emphasis on the people and things in your home that you love. Your home can be a place where your family will return after a long day at work or to relax with you on weekends.

It's the perfect spot to go out

A minimalized house is not only a great home to call your own, but it can also be a great place from which to travel. By not buying so much stuff and not spending money on repairs and maintenance, your funds will be more available. Joshua Becker called this the "minimalist income!"

This is money that can be used for many other purposes. It's important to remember that living in a small home will mean that you spend less time organizing, cleaning, and taking care your possessions. Instead, you'll have more time and energy to think about the future and plan. With all this extra money and time, you'll face the world prepared.

You can focus on the material and less on possessions

A majority of the things that we surround ourselves with are only distractions. Money cannot buy happiness, but comfort is all it can buy. We're constantly bombarded with promises of happiness via materialistic means whenever we turn on the TV or use social media. This adds to our anxiety and struggles every day.

You have to resist the urges that will make you unhappy. While it's hard to avoid the consumerism trap you must always remind yourself that it's just an illusion of happiness.

It gives you more peace and happiness

To hold on to possessions can only cause stress, as we'll be afraid of losing them. Simplifying your life will help you to let go of most of your possessions. This will allow you to feel calmer and more peaceful.

Decluttering can help you find the things you value most. You'll be happier in your life. It allows you recognize the false promises made by clutter in your life. By refocusing your priorities, you can find happiness and greater efficiency.

A cleaner, more pleasant environment

There will be less clutter in your house if there are fewer things. This makes it easier to clean up your house. It's also easier to move around the house if it is minimalist. Recall that the less things we consume (that don't really matter) the less harm we do to the environment by reducing the emissions from various products we don't use.

Help give your kids better life lessons

These valuable life lessons may not be taught to children in media. But if you and your family create a minimalist environment with your children (which they will soon learn), you are teaching them valuable lessons that they will carry with them for their entire lives. A minimalist home saves you the temptation to own more in order to maintain the comparison game, and it still makes your home more attractive. You are not bound to the past. However, you can release the past to make way for a better future.

Chapter 3: Lifestyle Habits For Minimalist Living

You can create a minimalist house in no time. It takes only one large sweep to get rid all the clutter from your home over the years. Maintaining minimalism over a long period of time can be challenging.

Why? It doesn't matter how frequently or thorough you do a home decluttering, clutter can quickly build up and sneak in. Before long, your home will be back to its original state of chaos and clutter.

It is important to have good minimalist habits and incorporate minimalism into your everyday life. These are some mindful habits that can help you maintain a minimalist atmosphere at home.

Wash your dishes as soon as you use them. Do not delay washing your dishes. You will find yourself with a sink full before you realize it. Two key minimalist benefits of washing dishes immediately after use are:

* Less dishes are needed than if dirty dishes are left in the sink to be washed later.

* Your kitchen will have a clean, organized appearance at all times.

Get rid of junk from your countertops every day. You could have organized all your kitchen equipment, beauty products, or other items neatly onto the respective countertops. Excessive display of items can make your home appear cluttered and messy, even though it is possible to arrange them neatly on the countertops.

You can make a minimalist habit of putting things away in the cabinets and drawers when you're done using them. The key element to minimalism is empty space.

For regular decluttering, divide your home into small spaces. The idea of spring cleaning your house can seem daunting. Do not let this stop you from living a minimalist lifestyle. It's a good habit to tidy up your home.

You can make a habit of dividing up your home into smaller areas. One small space at time, and then declutter it and clean that area only. Next, go to the next smaller space. The difficult but highly rewarding habit of breaking down elephantine portions into bite-sized pieces and eating one bite at time is something you should try to infuse in every part of your home, particularly in minimalism. These tips will help you to develop this essential habit.

* Choose a day that's convenient for you.

* Start with a small area. You could, for instance, focus on one kitchen cupboard.

* Take at least 15-20 minutes to clean up your chosen cabinet

* Take 5 minutes to rest

* For the next 15-20 minute, move to the next cabinet.

* Take another 5-minute rest.

* Keep going with the same steps until you see the fruits of your labor.

Take photos of the room before and afterwards. Focusing for just 15 minutes a day will show you the extent of what you can achieve. Your positive experiences and the results you see will motivate you to keep working on this decluttering habit.

It is important to get rid of all unopened mail right away. This truth is obvious if you look back at your own life. How many unsolicited bills, letters, and junk mail did you throw out in every painful decluttering effort only to have new mail clutter every empty space in your home? Sounds familiar?

Even if you did it only once a month or once a weekly, you're likely to be faced with a huge pile of mail. The thought of having to go through an awful lot of routine, but important mail can lead to procrastination. This is why it's important to get into the habit of sorting through your mail as soon you receive it.

The process of sorting your mail every day takes just a few minutes. You can sort your mail in a few minutes. You can scan and store important mail in soft copies. Trash or recycle the hard copies, especially those that are not critical.

Be strict with what you bring in to your home. Minimalism is all about keeping only the most essential things in your home. You can maintain a minimalist living space by exercising strict control over what you allow into your home.

Space is precious and beautiful. It is not only less effective to reduce minimalism but also decreases your work in maintaining a clean home. Here are some tips for controlling what you allow into your home.

* Do not allow relatives to dispose of things in your home. Don't be tempted to gift gifts for special occasions from family or friends. Send them a list with life experiences like tickets to movies, dinner coupons, and other memorable moments. Do not buy material objects that just add clutter to your home.

After deciding that you need the item, it will take 24 hours to pay online.

Accept only the things that you truly care about and recognize that they are useful for your home.

All the elements listed above can be used to form habits. It is important to practice the habits regularly in order to create them. When you feel overwhelmed by the lack of progress in cleaning up and decluttering, remember the numerous benefits.

You shouldn't let temporary setbacks derail you from your pursuit of minimalism. Look deep within to find the courage and strength to move on from temporary setbacks. Failures can serve as stepping stones for success and help you learn important lessons. Failures and setbacks don't have to be the end. These are just a few of the many turns you'll face in your life. But if you persevere through them, you will find success. Minimalism can be a lifestyle choice that reaps many benefits.

Chapter 4: Minimalist Home Decor

Extreme Minimalist

People often think of minimalism as frugal and cold. However, this is not the truth. Minimalism can be as simple or complex as you choose to make it. You may find that a single person living in a one-bedroom apartment has all they need. You may have a busy schedule and not have the time to clean your home every day. You might be able to save a dollar so that you can buy your house. But that is just one example. High-quality furniture can make a home feel warm and inviting. They don't save their money and instead spend it on the things that make life more joyful, such as a vacation. They only purchase what they are required and leave the rest to spend on what they truly love. Depending on your personality and how you live, where you end up on the spectrum depends on who you are. Your home will differ if you have children. Minimalism isn't about sacrificing things you love or treasure. It is about making your home and finances easier so that you can do what you love rather than what you have to.

Some people will feel pressured to go to extremes in minimalism. The pressure of society telling you to buy more, and then telling your to sell everything you have can make it difficult for you feel overwhelmed. This pressure should not force you to be a minimalist. You don't have to downsize or live in one-room apartments with only 20 items. Some people may have less. Some people don't care as much about luxury goods, while others do. There's nothing wrong with wanting nice things. This lifestyle does not have to be excessive. You can make minimalist living work for you. This will allow you to still feel like you.

This guide and tips will help you design a minimalist home.

Here are some tips to help you design a minimalist-friendly home. Here are some tips to help you design a minimalist home.

You can design one room at a time

When you're decluttering your entire home, it is best to only focus on one area when designing the room. It is easy to get overwhelmed if you attempt to design the whole house at once. Sometimes you just want to do it quickly because you're in a hurry. It's not the best approach to designing your house. Let yourself take your time to focus on one area and then move onto the next. Design regrets are not something you want. You can also think about a particular style and mood when designing. Next, you should design your individual rooms to reflect the style. This will make it easy to avoid rooms clashing.

Get timeless pieces

It is part of living minimalistically that you must constantly clean out your home and make changes to your decor as needed. We all want to follow trends and look trendy and modern. However, if a trend ceases, you no longer look trendy and are not in tune with the times. This can be avoided by selecting furniture and decor pieces which are timeless. So your home will never look outdated and modern. It is much easier to donate clothes that are not in style.

Start with Furniture

The furniture is what people first notice when they enter a property. The furniture is the most important part of a room. Next, you should focus on accents and decor. It's important to realize that furniture is your largest investment in your home. Try to keep your furniture in line with your color palette. It doesn't mean that you have to get new couches or chairs. It's possible to use couch covers to achieve the look you desire. You can change the couch covers to achieve the look you desire five years later.

Take Your Things Out of sight

Minimalist homes are meant to be beautiful and show off your nice decor. Your child's kindergarten macaroni art is not included in this minimalist home. It's not wrong to show your children off. However, you should do it right. One way is to put them in a collage and then hang them on your walls. It's important to store your stuff away from view so you can keep the items that matter most and not display them.

Edit and Remove

There will be three types of piles as you go through your home: keep, donate and toss. As you decide where to put an item, you can always place it in an unidentified pile. These are your belongings; it is okay to give yourself time to make changes. Minimalism is not something you should do overnight. It is possible to re-evaluate your decisions and see if the items you kept are still necessary. You'll notice this most in the kitchen with items you thought you would use but didn't. You should be open-minded when decluttering your home. If necessary, you can go through them twice.

Function is the most important thing

There is no reason to have pieces just because there might be twenty people in your home. Take a look at your daily functions and see what you really require. If you only need one person, then there is no need for multiple chairs and couches. You can buy a sofa or a sectional and then divide it up when company arrives.

Clean Lines

Furniture should be straight and clean. Avoid pillows that are too round and susceptible to falling off. To give your room a contemporary look, choose sleek pieces that are modern in style.

Opt For Neutral Walls

Your walls shouldn't have any bright colors. It's a good idea to choose neutral colors such as white or soft-toned brown. You can add color by using throw pillows or a rug in the room.

Toned down Floors

Don't be afraid to show off hardwood floors. You don't need to cover the floor with multiple mix match rugs. A hardwood floor in your home can be a wonderful way to warm it up. It also highlights how beautiful the flooring is. You can also create a comfortable atmosphere by using wood as a surface.

Let Nature's Light In

Embrace your windows. You should clean your windows both from the inside and out. The goal is to let as much sunshine in as possible. To ensure that there is enough light entering your home, don't place heavy furniture right in front.

Mirrors are a great way to make space more open

Mirrors can help you make your space appear larger if it is smaller. Although this is an old trick it's a good one.

Simple Lighting

Be smart about your lighting. Ten lamps are not necessary in one room. If you place the bulb in the right wattage so it can shine throughout the room, then you will have enough lighting.

Use furniture as a Decoration

You can decorate your home with your furniture. A unique chair can become the focal point in your home. Then you can design the rooms around it. This is a wonderful way to use the furniture pieces that you already own.

Shelving can be vertical

Vertical shelves make a great choice for shelving. Vertical shelving will make your room seem taller. They are more compact and take up less space. These can be purchased in white or you could choose to decorate with warm, bright colors.

Textured Fabrics Give You Warmth

If the neutral color scheme is making your space too cold, throw pillows, blankets, and rugs can be used to add warmth. If you are looking to improve a boring, uninteresting wall, a textured wallpaper can be a good option.

Combining Storage and Decoration

You should always have storage space in your rooms. However, you don't want to use a bookcase and bins. For a room that looks organized and complete, combine decorative pieces like wooden containers.

Eliminate Hardware

If possible, your lights should be suspended from the ceiling. As with any drawers. The built-in handles on top of dressers will allow you to keep the room's lines clean and reduce any contrast.

Chapter 5: Cleaning The Clutter - Donating Is Caring

Minimalists know that decluttering is an essential part of minimalism. It makes you more aware, helps you see the bigger picture, and helps to keep your space organized. Many people aren't sure where to start when it comes decluttering their spaces. It is easy to feel overwhelmed by how many items or the mess in our homes. If you follow a plan, decluttering can be done. To avoid becoming overwhelmed by your space, it is important to follow a stepby-step procedure. The easier it is to declutter and clean, the better. You want to make cleaning fun and enjoyable. Cleaning is often considered boring and uninteresting.

However, I want you to see how much fun it can be. Part of minimalism is learning how to enjoy small tasks such as cleaning. Learning to love cleaning will help you create a plan and effectively manage your space. The best way to manage clean is to schedule a day for cleaning. A cleaning plan or system can help you organize your space and keep it clean. We will discuss the advantages of cleaning and regularly giving away things that you no longer need. Clearing clutter can help you make your space reflect your lifestyle. You can also learn how to clear your thoughts and reduce clutter.

Cleaning and Decluttering

This is the third step of your minimalism journey. This will help you clear out clutter and help you understand the importance of living in clean surroundings. Start by decluttering. Identify the importance and function of each space. The purpose of each space will help you organize it. Ask yourself what the room is meant for and what it's used for. If your living area is intended to be used for entertaining, lounging and watching TV, you need to ensure that it facilitates these activities. The same goes for bedrooms that are used as workspaces or exercise areas. What are you looking for in your space? This will allow you to identify what items can be kept or thrown away. Overcrowding and hoarding are when items are placed where they aren't needed. If the item is not appropriate for the space, you can either repurpose it or place it in another area. Allow yourself to take a walk through your space. You should also consider how each item makes you feel, as well as whether it serves its purpose. After creating your list you can start to plan what areas you should clean. This will help you ensure that every item is serving its purpose.

Selecting one space at the time is key to cleaning out your space. Pick one room or section in your home. Once you have identified the area you want, organize your items into three piles. The first includes items you're keeping, while the second contains items you are donating. The final pile includes items that will be given to friends or loved ones. This helps you identify your belongings. Keep in mind your space's purpose and start organizing one item at the time. Then, choose an item to organize and ask yourself these questions:

* Is this item appropriate for this space?

* Do I require this item?

These questions allow you to determine whether or not you really need the item. If you choose to keep it, then make sure that it is placed in the right spot. Do this for each room in your home. Assess your kitchen space, cabinet by cabinet, when you're arranging it. You can organize your belongings into three categories. This process is applicable to all areas of your home. Once you have sorted all your belongings, take the time to look at what you plan on keeping. Are the things you keep necessary? Does the item serve a purpose or are they unnecessary? It is important to assess your belongings again in order to reduce their clutter. Your donations and gifts can be put aside to later be organized in the location you prefer.

Once you have assessed all areas of your home, you can begin cleaning. The first stage was to declutter and identify the things you need. Prepare your home for new living arrangements and ways of organizing your clutter during the clearing and cleaning stage. Cleanliness makes you feel intentional and purposeful. As with decluttering, focus on one space at a given time. It may be the first time you have deep cleaned your space, depending on your lifestyle. Clear the area you want to clean from all items. Once you have done this, use a damp cloth along with a cleaning detergent to clear any dirt or dust.

It is important to clean your space before you begin any change. A clean space can make your space feel brighter and help you feel more confident about the changes that you are making. Before organizing your belongings in the space, clean out each room. You might discover that not all of the items you planned to put in the space are possible. If this is the case, you might want to consider storage containers or further minimizing items you wish to keep. In my experience, it was best to place as few items as possible in each section. Also, make sure to leave enough space between each item in your cabinets. This will help you avoid overcrowding and ensure a visually appealing product.

Apart from keeping your space clean and tidy, cleaning has other benefits. Cleanliness can improve your health and strengthen your immune system. Living in a clean home can lower your chance of suffering from allergies. Keep your home orderly and keep germs and bacteria at bay by scheduling weekly cleanings. Avoid using detergents that negatively impact your environment or your health (Olapade, 2019). Your creativity will be boosted by cleaning out your space. Consider how you'll use the space after cleaning. It can help you envision how to arrange your space.

Cleansing your home or apartment can make you feel happy and energized. It gives you a sense that you are in control of your space. This is important in minimalism. Finally, having a clean space will improve your mood and allow you to concentrate on the task at hand.

Learning how to manage clutter in your house is essential. This is important for minimalism because it helps to organize your home and reduce clutter. Here are some tips to help you manage your space.

* Decluttering your home and environment is not enough. Also, manage your time. Make time to relax and create a schedule that helps you get your tasks done. You need to strike a balance between productivity & relaxation. It will make you feel happy and help reduce stress. Declutter your mind. Prioritize what you eat. It is important to set aside time to care for your mental health and your physical well-being.

Find creative ways to store your products. Your home doesn't need to be identical to other peoples. To add storage to your home, you might consider installing wall hooks or floating and invisible shelves. Your space should not feel cluttered. Hang hooks should be placed vertically or horizontally to create a minimalist appearance in your home. This ensures consistency in your home and gives it a minimalist look (Garrity. 2020).

* Make your space more organized by using storage systems to organize your drawers, cabinets, and other items. To maintain order in your space you can purchase organizers and dividers. You can organize your kitchen and drawers by adding simple storage containers or dividers. The storage solution you choose should be appropriate for the space. You can use labels to help you label and organize your belongings. Organisers are a good option, but don't overload your space (Lifford. n.d.). This tip is cost-effective if you make your own storage solutions using cardboard. This drawer uses a homemade organizer to organize artist's pencils.

Donations

Donating is a great way of reducing your number of items while also benefiting someone or a cause. Donating can be a way to give items you already own to an individual or charity. This is essential for minimalism. It shows your ability and willingness to help others. You need to admit that certain items do not serve you. Consider donating items you no longer need or possess to avoid duplicates. As I discussed the importance of decluttering your home, I advised that you work one room at time and create three piles: items you want to keep and things to give. It is essential that you label your belongings before you donate. This will allow you to track what you are giving and ensure it goes to its right place.

Donating gives you the opportunity to be fulfilled by helping others. It is comforting to know that your belongings have been repurposed or used. It is much better than to let your belongings sit in dust or unused. You can donate both new and gently used items. Recognize the fact that you don't need to have multiple shirts or countless pairs of jeans. Donate your old items so that someone else can use them. Sometimes the jeans you don't wear often can become a favorite in someone else's closet. Give your friends and family a chance to see your gifting options. This ensures they get items they actually use. You don't want to gift an item they can't use, or something that will sit in their house collecting dust. Your parents will be able to shop through your possessions, making gifting even more fun.

Don't forget that not all items you don't need anymore can be donated to someone else. It is important to assess the quality of the item and determine its place. I always consider whether it would be a comfortable item to receive the item I am donating. This is a quick way to see where your donations need go. I feel comfortable knowing the items that I am donating are not damaged or worn out. Giving helps to keep you grounded and set a good example for your loved ones. You can share the joy of giving with your friends and family, inspiring them to do the exact same. This will help you encourage minimalism in others, without making them change. It is a great way to show your children the value of giving and set a positive example. CanadaHelps, n.d., encourages children to give up old clothes, toys and books. Donating is a way to learn the value of giving up. It encourages one to let go of material possessions and reminds another to be grateful for what they do have.

Practice donating your time as well as your belongings. When organizations receive donated items, they will need your help in sorting them out and distributing them. Depending on your cause, you might be asked to donate your time or help with cleaning, cooking, and just enjoying time with people. Charity organizations value your time. As opposed to volunteering during peak times like Christmas, consider volunteering with organizations when there is no holiday. Find out about the causes and charities in your area before you decide which charity or organization you would like to donate. This is important when you are donating larger goods. You can pick an organization based on the causes and beliefs that you believe in. By looking at their past work, and where the donations went, I recommend that you research the places you would like to donate. This will ensure that your items are effective used and benefit your cause. Make sure you research the items that are accepted by your cause to ensure that they are properly used. Minimalist minimalism is fun and you should practice it as much as you can. Don't keep things that you don't use or need anymore.

Chapter 6: How To Declutter Your Home

The workplace is not the only place we spend our time, but the home is the most important. A messy home can lead to stress and anxiety. It is important to start in one room first before moving on to the next. We will discuss strategies to help you de-clutter each room in your house.

How to Clear the Living Room of All Things

The living room can be used by all members of the family for entertainment, work, and play. If a family begins to live there, any organized or preplanned design could be a great idea. You can easily become overwhelmed by the clutter in your living room. Here's how to get rid of clutter in your living room.

* Talk with everyone

First, sit down with your family and share your visions for the space. Talk to your children about how important it is for them to keep their toys out of the living space. You might consider having a home-office in one corner of your living room if you have a coffeetable full of bills. To ensure everything is put in its proper place, plan ahead.

* Get rid any items that aren't being used

You should take stock of everything in your living area to determine which items you want to keep. The sentimental items you have in your family's possession should be kept. If you have any other items, ask if anyone in your home has used them within the past year. If you are not satisfied with the answer, it is best to donate or discard them. If you don't think the item will fit in your living space, find another place to put it.

* Need storage solutions?

Place your valuables out of sight. Also, make sure you have a display spot for any decorative items. There are furniture pieces that can double as storage. For example, tables that have drawers, media cabinets or benches with doors. A specific shelf or drawer can be used for items that are connected to the activity of the living area. For example, you could place the remote controls and craft materials in the media cabinets. Use floating shelves or display cabinets to store decorative items. They will be visible from all sides and won't move.

* Stay organized

After clearing out the clutter and getting organized, it is the responsibility of each member of the family to keep the area tidy. It is important to use your living room for the purposes you have planned. You can also use other rooms for different activities. This will make sure that clutter doesn't get from the kitchen, bedroom, or home office. Your family should remind you to return all items to where they came from after you have done with them. You will only need a few moments to empty the space, with the help and support of each family member.

How to Clear Out the Kitchen Cabinets

The best way to clear out your kitchen cabinets is to get rid of any unused or forgotten items. You'll need a trash can, an empty bin, or a damp rag you can move around with. You will need to open each cabinet individually, starting with the top. Toss all garbage into the trash bags. You can also remove any objects that may be out of place. Rearrange the rest. You can wipe away any spillages with a clean rag before drying the area. Keep going until each cabinet is cleaned up. You can take your bin out and place everything in its correct place.

You might want to understand why the plastic container is better than simply placing things in their correct place. You're more likely to return things to their rightful storage space if it is in another cabinet or pantry than if your stuff is on the countertop.

How to Declutter Your Bathroom

Are you stressed about your bathroom clutter? Are you frustrated that you are unable to find the right items? It is sometimes hard to imagine how small spaces such as bathrooms can get cluttered. It can take between 15 and 20 minutes to declutter a bathroom, depending on its size and the time it took you to do it. It's important to get rid of all the clutter, including the drawers, countertops, and the space under the sink. This will allow you to quickly locate what you need when you wake up in the morning.

To clean out your bathroom you'll need a trash container, a timer and a recycling bin. The hamper should be placed at the front of the bathroom. If you have dirty hand towels you can change them with fresh ones from the linen closet. Transfer any laundry to the hamper if you have it. Toss or recycle any items that are not needed, such as used tissue and toiletry handles. You can place any items that are not in your room into the place-all bag, bin or container. This includes jewelry, shoes and clothing. Take out any loose items and clean up the sink.

Consider storing the jewelry you wear every day in the bathroom if it is difficult to find. This should be done for both your drawer and under your sink. Make sure to get rid of items that aren't rightfuly there. If an item keeps appearing in a different place, it is time to find a home. It would be best to place your makeup brush in a sink, rather than putting it out of reach. Your hamper can be taken and placed in the laundry room.

De-Cluttering Linen Closets

Nothing is more messy than a linen closet. A linen closet can be pictured as a collection of heavy towels and sheets, plus comforters, pillows, and tablecloths. You can place things you no longer need, but will need in the linen closet. These items can include sheets and extra towels. You'll most likely have to use the existing line cabinet in your home. However, if the closet is already occupied you can still use it as a storage space.

After you have gathered everything into a pile, decide whether you want them to be kept, donated, or thrown away. Keep in mind that you can donate the items that you don't use or haven't used to benefit another person. Don't keep things that you don't use anymore. If you do not have a closet equipped with shelves or drawers, you might consider buying a storage box. They will allow you to organize your belongings and not just throw them around.

A linen closet should contain basic items such as bath towels, sheets, toiletries, and bed sheets. You can place more items in a linen closet if you have enough space. Your goal is to make it easy to find your items and retrieve them. Don't let the linen closet become a dumping ground for products you don't use.

Chapter 7: Simple Ways To Stay Healthy For Decades

You want health, longevity, good health, and a high quality of living. You do not wish to feel in pain, suffer from diseases or suffer from other conditions. We all desire that.

There is so much to know about being healthy. These exercises, eating these superfoods, taking these supplements, and doing cleanses and detoxes are essential. Although some of your health issues are out of your control, such as being disabled, it is possible to control what you can do.

In truth, it is very easy to remain healthy. For many thousands of year, human beings have managed to stay healthy. To be successful in managing your health, it doesn't require a doctorate. You only need to have some common sense, and a few basic tools.

This chapter focuses on how to maintain your health and be healthy in today's modern world using your common sense, smart habits, and common sense. It doesn't matter if you have expensive equipment or need to take supplements. It is enough to understand some common sense principles that will help you make smart decisions about your overall health.

The western world takes the body for granted as its default. We eat whatever we please, even fast food. So out of shape are many of us that a stroll around the mall is considered exercise. To drink alcohol or use drugs, "a night off" is what we consider to be "a night of work". We're then shocked when we don't sleep well, wake up stressed and feel like s #&%..

It is intuitively obvious that pets need to be fed, exercised, and slept in order to thrive. It is also important for you to have it. People don't always take care of their pets as well as they give to themselves. They will take home bags of expensive cat food, and let their cat enjoy it while they have a twenty-cent bowl ramen.

It is easy to learn the fundamental rules of caring about a human's body. While scientists continue to refine their knowledge, the fundamentals of human health and well-being are known. The good news? Caring for your body isn't difficult, nor expensive, nor time-consuming. Start by learning a few selfcare habits.

Real Food

You wouldn't put diesel in a Ferrari. The problem is that we consume processed foods. This makes it difficult to make high-efficiency, high-quality machines. Amazing things can be done if you have the right fuel. The wrong fuel can cause sputtering, a seized motor and even a complete engine shutdown.

Many people will attempt to convince you that they have a perfect diet plan. Eat keto, whole30, or paleo. These diets might be useful for people who are following them.

But, you don't need to adhere to any diet to be healthy. An index card contains the essential rules for food and you don't need a university education.

In Defense of Food, Michael Pollan is a food journalist who outlines these easy-to-remember guidelines about food.

Eat food.

Not too much.

Mostly plants.

Although they may appear so easy that it is silly, these rules conceal powerful truths about the human diet.

Eat food. It seems easy, right? The truth is that most people aren't actually eating food. Pollan says that we are eating edible food-like substances. Anyone who has ever eaten Twinkies will know what that means. You don't have to be told by anyone else whether you're eating food. It's already obvious. Food makes you feel full, or satisfied. Twinkies are not a satisfying food.

Don't eat so much. In communities where people don't eat beyond their limits, they are considered the most healthy. Moderation is encouraged in the most healthy communities. People should eat until they're full. Okinawa, Japan's island most known for its long-lived, healthy residents, practices hara hachi bun me, Confucius' teaching to eat only until you feel eighty percent full.

Mostly plants. Even though you may love steak, most people can't survive on a diet of domesticated meat. While wild game meat is still a viable option, there are many indigenous communities that rely solely on it. But there's a big difference in wild game meat from a bloody American steak. There is a significant difference in the way your body looks compared to that of an Indian wild game hunter. We can all thrive if our diets are mostly vegetables.

Move Your Body

One of my favorite writing aphorisms I use is "We discovered the fountain of youthfulness, and that's exercise." Although many people in the west complain about their various ailments and sufferings, most western diseases can be effectively treated or cured with exercise.

Research has shown that exercise can lower the chance of you getting any type of cancer. 1

Regular exercise is a good way to prevent heart diseases such stroke, metabolic syndrome, or high blood pressure.

Exercise regularly can also help with arthritis, type 2, diabetes, and fall injuries. 2

Exercise is just as effective in treating depression than antidepressants. Combining both of these treatments creates an extremely powerful mental health treatment. 3

You don't need to make exercise complicated, just as with eating. Although you may be able to exercise three times a week at a gym, that doesn't mean you need to do it every time. While there are different physical activity levels recommended by the CDC for different ages, everyone is different 4. My rule is to move your body until tired.

It is not a good idea to move your body until it becomes boring. This is the most common thing people do at the gym. They do a few reps, feel a little tired, and then they say to themselves "Wow, what an amazing workout!" You must do this. They're not seeing the alleged benefits of exercise and wonder what they are. Move until your muscles are exhausted.

Moving until you are exhausted means that you have to move until you lose your ability to maintain your good form. Your legs will feel like jelly if you are running. Jump until your feet hurt the next day. Do it until you are exhausted from whatever activity you're engaging in.

The beauty of this standard, however, is that it can meet you wherever you are. The benchmark for "tired" if you are an elderly person, disabled, or someone who is recovering from injury will be a walk down the street. You might be a physically gifted young man that hasn't gotten up in a while. You shouldn't push yourself past some set of standards that might not be right for you. Push yourself until your tired.

My favorite thing about this philosophy? I don't need weight tracking. I don't need to have a specific plan to increase or decrease my physical activity. All I need is to listen and follow my body's lead. Every time my body tells me its limits, I can just listen.

Mental health patients may have difficulty moving their bodies. This is not surprising as depression is considered an "invisible impairment" by many doctors. It often causes significant problems with motivation and energy. Even though exercise may seem difficult or impossible when you're feeling depressed you can reap the rewards of your efforts if the effort is put in.

Even if depression doesn't strike, physical activity is vital for your mental health. When you feel low, it can be hard to get up from your bed. This is normal. These are times when your exercise is not a priority. It doesn't matter if you can't say, "I did my best today," it will make you feel better.

Good Sleep

Many people don't really understand sleep and why it is so important. Not just losing consciousness each night, sleep is much more. Sleep is a unique physiological state. Our brains switch from maintaining general consciousness to producing two different types sleep cycles during sleep: NREM or REM. Each sleep cycle is associated a particular type of brainwaves. These waves do not occur when our brains are unconscious due to alcohol consumption, anesthesia, and taking sedatives. Only natural sleep cycles can produce healthy waves in the brain.

These sleep cycles have a major impact on our health. They affect every part of the body, including the brain and colon. They affect our cognitive ability and mental health as well as our digestion, immune system and heart health. Sleep is an essential biological requirement that supports the overall functioning of the body.

It's even worse that even one hour of proper, organic sleep every night can have significant effects on one's ability to function. Even a single hour of sleep loss can result in memory loss, cognitive issues, increased appetite and weight gain, as well as decreased energy levels. Research has shown that drivers who get only a few hours sleep per night are as impaired in driving as drunk drivers.

You wouldn't be foolish to get adequate sleep if you want to make the most of your time and do what you love.

Before we go any further, let us discuss how caffeine works. Without talking about caffeine, it's impossible to talk of sleep. Here's how caffeine works. The brain builds up a chemical called Adenosine every night that one is not sleeping. Every night during sleep, the brain excretes adenosine. Caffeine causes us to feel awake as it blocks the brain from feeling adenosine. The brain doesn't feel the adenosine anymore but it continues building up in the body. Caffeine crashes are caused by caffeine. When the caffeine wears out, the brain no longer feels the adenosine. All the adenosine in your body is crashing back into your consciousness. Caffeine cannot replace sleep. It can, however, temporarily delay it.

Dr. Matthew Walker is a neuroscientist who has written Why We Sleep. He offers two questions to help you assess if you get enough sleep.

"First, after getting up in the morning, are you able to fall asleep at ten or eleven? If the answer to this question is "yes", it's likely that you are not getting enough quality and quantity of sleep.

"Second. Can you function optimally in the morning without caffeine?" If your answer is no, then you're most likely self-medicating for chronic sleep deprivation.

Sleep does not accumulate a debt. While your body is still suffering from sleep deprivation, the long-term effects can be severe. It is essential that you get enough sleep every night to be able to manage your health responsibly.

Dr. Walker states that getting good sleep is as simple as going to bed at the same time every morning. The biological clock is something that the body can't change, especially on an everyday basis. An irregular sleeping schedule is a sign of sleep deprivation.

Another thing you can control is how much daylight you get. The more sun you receive during the day the better. To get a good night's rest, you should limit your exposure to light after sunset. Although it's possible to have a very dark environment after sunset, this is not the best lifestyle. Settle for keeping your environment dim. Smart bulbs can be set up to automatically turn redder and darker as night falls. Configure all screens to turn redder and dimmer as the day progresses. Turn all screens off at least an hour before you go to sleep.

You may also find it difficult to fall asleep after noon caffeine. Caffeine can stay in your body for up to six hours, depending on which individual. Any caffeine intake will disrupt your body's ability and brain function to fall asleep. If you can't fall asleep in the evening, and you drink caffeine after 2:45 p.m., then you may have a caffeine problem.

It is possible to trick people into believing they have sleeping problems by drinking alcohol. Alcohol makes you fall unconscious, not asleep. It is not a good sleep aid. Anyone with sleep disorders must quit drinking alcohol before they are diagnosed.

Last but not most, melatonin isn't going to make you sleep more soundly, but it may help you sleep more on a set schedule. Melatonin, a hormone that prepares the brain for sleep, is one example. While it has not been shown to improve sleep quality or cure insomnia, research shows that it helps with jetlag and maintaining a consistent sleep schedule. Take melatonin one hour and a tenth before bed if your sleep schedule is irregular. You will find it easier to fall asleep when it is right for you.

Chapter 8: Decluttering In Your Home

Once you've cleared out larger areas of your home, it is time to decide if you want declutter by area or by category. I find it easier to be productive if I only tackle one room at once and move on when the task is done. Below are some suggestions for cleaning out certain rooms in your home. There are many great methods that can be used to declutter a specific area of your home.

Kitchen

If you have received any souvenir gifts from your travels by family and friends, such postcards. Keyrings. Magnets. Glasses. These items are great, but if these items aren't used or looked at often, they can just become clutter. You have the option of keeping or getting rid of souvenirs.

Ordering takeout often comes with a takeout order menu, coupon codes for next order, promotional magnets as well as packets of sauces or spices, napkins and cutlery. These items rarely serve a purpose as we live in an era of digital technology where we can easily search online for promotions and menus. It is likely that we have our own cutlery or dish towels which can be used instead of disposable napkins.

Keep any coupons that are still valid, put them in your bag or wallet. You will be able to use the coupon instead of laying around. You can also get rid most sauces and other spices that come with meals. Most sauces and spices you have in your kitchen already aren't necessary.

Containers that don't fit properly, have broken lids or are missing their lids tend not to be thrown out. These items should be sent to the recycling center if they are still in use. You should also consider switching to glass containers instead of plastic. Plastic is susceptible to odors and can be thrown out when it becomes less useful. Glass containers can be cleaner and last longer than plastic. It is also less harmful to the environment than

plastic.

Sauces may be expired or not what you are looking for. It is worth taking the time to look through your sauces, and getting rid of anything you are not using or past their expiration date. If you find any spices or fragrant herbs in your spice drawer that have lost flavor or are expired or you don't use, you should get rid of them. It is best to keep spices for between 6-12 months before replacing with fresher ones.

As you go along your daily life, you will acquire many different small appliances. Look through your appliances and determine which ones are still being used, which have not been used for more than one year, and where there are other appliances that serve the same purpose. If appliances are in good shape, they can often be sold or donated to a family that might be in need.

After many years of use, dish towels become worn, stained, and dirty. Even worse, you might have a dishtowel that is brittle from being left near the stove top. Most often, these dish towels are kept in our emergency stash for times when we don't need them. These old towels should be thrown out or used as a cleaning cloth to make new, stronger towels.

Cookbooks can take up lots of space. They are also heavy and bulky. Many of us buy cookbooks to learn how or discover new recipes. Think about how often you use your cookbooks.

I often search online for a particular recipe to follow while I cook. One or two books are most important to me. These cookbooks should be reliable and can complement my style. Look through your cookbooks, and decide if it is time to pare down your collection. We no longer need heavy cookbooks that take up space. It is possible to either sell or donate your cookbooks.

Food cans, which are large and heavy, can take up space in your food pantry. Check your cans for expired or unusable items. If the cans you are getting rid off have not expired, don't forget to drop them off at a drop-off location for those in need. You can also dispose off them if their expiration date is past.

Common Rooms

Like cookbooks, CDs/DVDs is another category that we don't use anymore. Nowadays, there is no need to own physical copies or DVDs. You can easily rent, purchase, stream or download music online. With so many download options available and so many different choices, you don't need a physical collection.

Go through all your CDs and DVDs. Make sure you check which songs you can download via iTunes. Then, only keep the items you value and cannot find anywhere else. Many people enjoy keeping rare and collectible movies and music. However, it is possible to make some money selling them.

Candles are one of those items that we rarely notice. We may not be able to tell when there is too much candle wax in a jar or when the candle can't be lit any more. You can go through your house to check for any candles that are not usable. If the candle was in a glass bottle, you can either reuse it or send to be recycled.

While your family might disagree, you will find that older gaming consoles take up lots of space and are rarely used, compared to the newer games and consoles. Many older console games have been remade and are now available online.

Many consoles are now equipped with no CD drive, so you can download and install any game you like right from their digital shop. It is now unnecessary to have physical copies of the games. Have a family meeting to discuss how you can get rid of your older consoles and games. Also, ask your loved ones if they are able to download their favorite games as digital copies. These consoles could be sold for extra money or given to loved ones.

Another item we forget to think about when we clean out our homes is cleaning supplies. You may find that a brand you like is not working for you. If this happens, keep the other brand in the back of your cupboard.

Clean out your cleaning supplies. Take out any that don't perform well or are duplicates.

Take your cleaning supplies with you when you are done.

If you have old electronics devices or computers, you can take them out of your home and give them to a computer shop. They will format the computer and wipe their contents. Once all data has been removed, the options are endless. You can sell or donate your devices to make extra cash, give them away to loved ones, or recycle them at a shop that deals in cellphones or computers.

I used to have six albums full of photos. This is a lot of photos, and many people have even more. Some people keep photos in a box or garage. Photos and albums take up much space and you never know where they might end up. It's a good idea for you to digitize your photos. Only keep the best and most sentimental photos. This allows you to have all of your photos at your fingertips. Additionally, you can create a shared online folder for the entire family that contains their memories and photos.

This is also true for receipts. To be able either to obtain the warranty on an item or return it to the store for a refund, you will need to digitize your receipts. You should first find out if the store requires a copy of your receipt to issue a return or warranty. I like to keep all my important receipts in a box in my bedroom.

This method allows you to go through your items and see which are expired. The return period for items is typically seven days. Some stores, however, allow you to return an item within thirty days.

If you find it difficult to find space for magazines or books, then you might also want to declutter your bookshelves. The bulky and heavy nature of novels, reference books, stacks of magazines, and other items can occupy lots of space. Decluttering your magazines and books will make space available for the important things.

You can give or sell any books that have been read or digital copies to someone who would enjoy them. It is no longer necessary to have physical copies of books in today's digital age. I get rid of all novels and search for digital copies through sites like Amazon. I don't keep any books other than reference books or novels that I love or have sentimental value.

Magazines are slightly more complex than books. Magazines will lose their content over time. Ask your family members if they would be interested in reading the magazine once you are done. Magazines can also serve as a resource for school projects. Magazines can't be sold. They are usually donated or thrown away when they are no longer needed.

Bedrooms

I know that I keep my old pillows on top my cabinet, but it is a habit I make. Instead of keeping the old pillows in your cupboard, ask your guests if they would like to bring their own pillows. Or get a special pillow for travel. Your pillows can be given to anyone who is able to use them. These pillows can be donated to a shelter for the homeless or an animal shelter.

Let's just be honest. There is a pair of boots you keep in your closet that aren't worn, but you probably won't wear. If your shoe collection has grown out of control and there is no room for new shoes, you can get rid of shoes that you don't use or are worn.

I love handbags. I like to rotate between wallets and handbags. But there are others that go unutilized in my closet. Sometimes I am surprised to find handbags I didn't even know I had. They weren't my favorite and I likely didn't use them again.

Don't keep any handbags or wallets that are no longer in use. It is time for you to purge your collection. Look through your handbag collection. You can keep up to four different bags that you can swap out and change as often as you like. I try to keep two trendy handbags, one that I use everyday and one that is more professional.

If you are not able to pare down your handbags to four, then make the best of it and come back later. You can sell, gift, or craft your handbags. If the handbag isn't in good condition or you are unable to use it for another purpose, you can throw it out.

You can also look through your jewelry while you are decluttering your purse and wallet collections. I love to store my jewelry in a special box. It looks great and is well organized. Unfortunately, I tend to collect way too many pieces.

Each piece of jewelry should be taken out. Take a look at how it feels and perhaps try it on. If the jewelry is not for you, if it doesn't fit you or if there are any broken pieces, you can dispose of it. You can replace it with jewelry you like. You can either give your jewelry away or sell it. If the jewelry is damaged you can reuse it for crafts or throw it away if it has no use.

While you're going through the bedroom, make sure you look through your shirts and skirts. I like to start by getting rid of all my clothes and then taking out the clothing that I want to try on to see if it fits. Get rid of clothing that does not fit or doesn't feel right for you.

Try to avoid asking the question "Am this something I will wear later after I have lost weight?" and "Am this something I'm going to wear when I go out?"

Use a method like the closet hanging method to determine which of your items you use within a specified time frame, such as three or four months. After doing this for several months, you will be able to see which seasonal items are most worn and what is not.

It is important to eliminate anything that is damaged, worn out, thinned, stretched, or stained as part of your wardrobe declutter. You can either donate or sell clothing that is still in good shape. It is difficult to sell clothes, but I have found it works well. You can use them to make crafts or cut them into rags for cleaning. If you are unable to use the item for another purpose, and it is in poor condition, you can just throw it out.

Also, scarves and tie can be hanged on the closet rack using the same method. However you should mark them so that it is easy to see what you use. Otherwise, you can select your favourites and dispose of the rest. But socks are more challenging. It is a little more difficult to find socks that are missing. I keep mine in a box or wicker container at the top my cupboard. Don't keep your single socks or the tattered ones. These can be used as crafts or thrown away.

Chapter 9: Arranging And Decluttering Outdoors/Porch

A clean and tidy environment is more inviting, less stressful, and more enjoyable. It is something we all recognize, but many overlook the fact that outside spaces can be just as messy. This makes it less likely that we will enjoy having large gatherings of friends or enjoying a relaxing day in our backyard. It makes our outdoor spaces more inviting and progressively functional. If you find yourself with too much stuff on your patio, these eight tips can help.

1. Arrange Your Outdoor Kitchen

Engaging is easier when the open-air kitchen is well-stocked. But a chaotic one will make it less inviting for visitors. You can keep all the kitchen basics you require, like corkscrews or bottle openers, within reach. Cabinet coordinators are available to help you organize your cabinets and store crates under the counter. If you're not engaging, your goal should be to leave nothing on the countertops of your outside kitchen. It will make your outside kitchen much more appealing, make it easier for you to clean, and keep dust off your useful supplies. It is remarkable that a well-organized space makes you more comfortable and allows you to take advantage of the outside areas you have.

A refreshment alcocator is a container that can hold cold drinks. You can also use it to store ice or cold drinks. Trays are a great way to serve tea, coffee, lemonade and other liquids without having to carry individual containers. This is, of course, better for the planet, so you also get additional focuses. It is also a good idea to have a basin, funnel, or other large container that you can fill up with ice. This will keep your surfaces clean and free from any water, carton soft drink boxes, or six packs.

A basin for wine tops and wine sticks is a wonderful reward. It will assist with cleaning up after your gathering and will keep your yard clean. You might also consider a second can, such as small, aluminium jars with tight fitting tops that are used for dry stockpiling. This is especially useful if you use a charcoal grill barbecue. This will enable you to keep your coals near your barbecue and far away. In between events, any instances of pop or water should be kept in an indoor or open air cooler, in your bathroom, in a cupboard outside your kitchen, or under your carport. Do not leave them on the counter. You can also use them as party supplies.

2. A Deck Box is a great place to keep cushions, blankets and accessories.

Deck boxes are an affordable way to keep essentials close at hand, even when not in use. The deck boxes can be used to keep basic items close at hand so your visitors don't have the hassle of looking for a cover or a book to light the candles. Toss covers and porch furniture pads can be stored in a wooden deck box. This helps to prolong their lives and keeps them clean between events. Your deck or yard will look cleaner if you store any unnecessary items in it. This makes it more inviting for you to relax and enjoy your outdoor space.

3. Establish a Gardening Center

While eager nursery workers will always be looking for fertilized soil, plant manure and other items, anyone with a normal property should have some cultivating equipment and supplies. This can cause us to end up with mulch on the fence, additional pots along the deck's edge, and cultivation apparatuses left in a pail. Make a station for cultivating your lawn. This will help you get rid of the mess. A capacity bureau, which is a preparing stool with a capacity area, works well for this purpose and offers both a workspace as well as an area to plant merchandise. An under-counter closet is the perfect place to store smaller pots and small packs of fertilized earth. You can increase this space by adding snares or peg boards to the entryways for hanging plant devices and other little things. You can also store larger amounts of soil or mulch in your shed, or even your carport, to keep them out of your living areas.

4. You can either hide your garden tools or get rid of them.

It is simple to clean up patio mess without the use of yard care tools. In the case of a fake lawn garden, or a deck, then you won't need your grass cutter again and can throw out this large piece of yard equipment. You may also have other gardening tools, such as an edger, aerator, and communicate spreader. In this case, you can take them out of your yard. Some property owners may find selling your yard for the disposal of a couple of other instruments or appliances to be outrageous. If this is the case, you should not leave garden tools and other useless tools around your house or move a large nursery hose up onto your yard.

Your visitors won't like to walk around with a push cart blocking the walkway. A tool that points toward a porch bench is just going to let you know that you have work to do every time you head outside to enjoy your morning cup of coffee. These devices are not only unattractive, but can also be dangerous. It is possible to keep them in a shed, or in a designated corner of your carport. If this isn't possible, put up a security fence on your terrace or in your yard. It will hide your devices and keep them safe from prying eyes. A shed is another option, but it will not take up much space in your yard. Many property owners require nursery hoses. It is something that we don't want to have to carry out to the yard every time we need to water our plants.

A nursery hose is essential for your daily life. It's also not practical to store in a carport or shed. It means it will be always connected to the water nozzle and ready to go, but won't take away from the beauty of your open-air living areas. You can achieve this best by buying a compartment designed specifically to hide your hose. This could be an attractive earthenware pot, or a well-designed reel with a spread that allows you to move your hose up and hide it away when it is not in use.

5. Expand Garage Space and Shed

This isn't about cleaning out your garage or shed. But clearing out clutter in one or both of these spaces could lead to your success in cleaning up the yard. This involves removing unwanted items, organizing what you want to keep, and finding creative ways to fit more stuff into the large stockpiling territory. This could include stockpiling racks which attach to the roof or stockpiling cupboards.

After you have removed all items from your carport, you will have space that you can use for garden instruments.

6. Shroud Your Garbage Cans and Recycling Cans

Large numbers of people have at least three waste containers. This includes a yard trash holder, a recycling compartment, and a garbage can. We must always take the jars from the lawn to the control. Then, after they have been purged, you need to check the patio. The recycling bin is an important item that we can't live without but aren't able to use at night. A better alternative is to put them behind a privacy screen in your backyard. It makes it much easier to take them out on the road each week.

Many mortgage holders do not have a space in their front yards large enough to house these jars. If you don't have a lot of visitors to your yard, and are not looking for them when you grill with your family, the next best option is to create a space in your side garden that is just outside your front door. To limit interruption and hide the messiness, you might have to place a security fence in the area where your lawn is closest to your outside living areas.

7. Take control of your Fire Feature Supplies

While open-air chimneys or fire pits don't need a lot of decorations, adding fire starters, wood pellets, matches and wood starters to your porch can take up space. You won't need these items to be stored in a shed, carport or garage. But you can still keep your fire place clean and tidy with the basic necessities close by. This can be done by buying an aluminium can with a lid that can store wood, matches, and kindling when you're not using it for cleaning out your outdoor fireplace. Another option is to keep all of your supplies and tools in a bucket. This can be placed near your fire pit or pulled out from your garden shed. Another option is to buy a deck box that has enough interior space for your wood and tools, but not in plain sight.

8. Include storage for toys, supplies and equipment for dogs, children and pools

It is likely that your backyard has extra clutter because of the swimming pool and children. While a small shed, or pool house, is best, smaller pool toys, and products, can be kept in a waterproof deck box. These boxes are basically the weather-resistant version of a storage bench or chest that you would use indoors to store extra storage. They can be used for dog toys, toys for children, and supplies for dog supplies. These large storage boxes can hold a tricycle or ride-on toy in an attractive and spacious design. You can store large bags or treats for dogs, ropes and balls, as well as your dog's bedding, in these storage boxes.

Chapter 10: The Benefits Of A Simple Life

What is the current state of your room, at home or at work?

Do you see clutter, or not?

Recycle. Reflecting on your items will help you decide if you still have a use for them or if they can be recycled. It is up to you to decide whether it should be donated, sold, or recycled.

Recycling offers many benefits at all levels. Recycling can be done with your thoughts, emotions, as well as all your actions throughout the day. The real benefit of minimalism (also known as simple living) is that you will see the value in it.

To learn the value that I and others can provide. Ability to Give

Human beings were born with the ability of giving and receiving. We have been grateful to receive and have always given. When we donate, recycle or sell things that are not of use to us, we recognize that they can be very valuable to others. People in need can have less material possessions.

One correct action has a lot to do and can multiply into a powerful energy that can be used in amazing ways.

Therefore, it is important to always appreciate what we are doing. You should also learn to value your actions and yourself. I currently have a guitar that I can't play or study, and it lies just like that. I had already planned to sell it. It will be appreciated more by someone who is passionate about playing the guitar. However, I am happy to say that after making these changes in my own life, music has become something I really love. It's all possible thanks to minimalism, and by working on myself.

This is where you will begin to see the value in your actions.

Keep Moving!

Minimalism is a way to teach us the wonderful lesson of moving on.

You move past your past. By moving on, you get rid of any accumulations that are not adding value to you life. Are you truly willing to stick with something that does not serve its purpose? I believe that all things in life are meant to be learned. But if we don't learn from our experiences, those mistakes and stop moving forward, we will never learn. How will this make you feel?

Finding yourself stuck in a situation is not a good idea. We have all accumulated stuff in our homes. Do you believe you will be able maintain this balance and sanctity of your mind and feelings?

Let go of something and you can move on to your next chapter of life. People feel hurt when they lose their headphones or laptops.

This is how you should think about it. You're not planning for tomorrow, but living in the past. While attachments and letting-go can be difficult, they are essential to living a happy life.

Organized - Finances Lifestyle, Health and Relationships

How did I manage finances? I let go of things that were not needed. I started living a simple and limited life. I only use what is necessary. So, my finances were automatically managed. After realizing that my needs were not too extreme and I was part of the community, I began to balance my budget and manage them well. Because I do what is most important to me, which I love doing, which I bring the Emotional Intelligence Development Program (EIDP) to children, teens, adults and adults, I can now earn less. This allows me to live a minimal minimalist life. I started saving even though my salary was less, and began living a more luxurious lifestyle. Music is a big part of it all. I am currently learning Tabla. I also enjoy playing flute. While reading books, I'm also on a spiritual quest to improve myself.

I now work hard and live life to the maximum. My lifestyle has transformed. I feel so light inside. Let go of the things that are limiting your life on all levels. You will learn to live the right kind of life. Reduced weight, proper eating habits and good time management have made a difference in my health. I gained a lot weight because I was unable to concentrate on my health. My health was terrible. My health reports were not encouraging. Today I am clear in my mind. In just 4 to 5 months, 8 kgs have been lost. I did not exert any effort and maintained my diet, my lightness, as well as my lifestyle. My relationships are much better and I feel more connected.

I'm happier when I have time to interact with my friends and family. I listen more.

How many of you have sat down with your parents to discuss your childhood memories?

I did it with mom. It was a wonderful experience sitting down with my mom to learn about her childhood, her struggles and her happiness.

Because I don't get to see my father as often now, I do so with my father quite often. Nowadays, we watch shows together, sit together and talk about the past, the future, and the present.

All things start within you. If I feel that something is not right for me, if there is a toxic relationship within me, then my ability to manifest well will be limited. I will not allow myself to communicate freely with my friends. Communication is essential for any relationship.

I have let go of my life, and am now working on myself, one step at the time. You will see the world differently once you accept minimalism and start living in it. You'll be free from worries.

You will then see the simple, tangible benefits I'm enjoying.

My finances are well managed, and I have addressed my insecurities. My lifestyle is balanced. My health is well-managed. There are no dependencies in my relationships.

It sounds easy. You have to put in the work. While it's not an easy task, once you decide to take control of yourself and accept your current situation, there is no stopping happiness and joy from coming into your life.

Chapter 11: Declutter And Promote Happiness

It doesn't need to be about the stuff you own. Decluttering your home and getting rid of unwanted possessions can help to flow into and benefit other areas of your life. However, it's important to also work to improve your overall well-being and encourage joy and happiness. Here are some tips to help you become more organized, feel happier and get rid of mental clutter.

Write down Your Thoughts

You can write down everything you think about on a piece or computer paper. It doesn't matter what you have in your head, you can write it down so you can keep it on hand and come back to it later. This can help you focus on the task in hand or on what is most important to you. When I'm not working, I keep a piece o paper on my desk. This allows me to write down any ideas that arise. I will examine the piece of writing after I'm done with my work and then deal with it when I have the chance.

Keep a Journal

Alternately, if this method doesn't suit you, consider keeping a diary. A journal will allow you to take notes throughout the day. This journal is helpful in sorting through all the emotions you feel. You can also keep track of the tasks and goals you want to reach.

Writing down an emotion in your journal can help you use it as a way to think back on what caused it. You can either write the causes down or think about them. Next, think of how you could've handled the situation more effectively.

Focus on the release of the emotion. This can be done by remembering a happy memory or thinking of something good. When the emotion is over, you can start writing down the word. Then, take deep breaths and move on to your day.

But your journal doesn't just have to contain negative feelings. If you feel happy about a day or someone who has made your day better, you can write a journal entry detailing what happened.

Next, if your mood is low or you are experiencing negative emotions, go back to the journal entries you made and reflect on what they did for you. By doing this, you can fill up your mind with positive emotions and forget all the negative feelings that have caused you anger.

Declutter Your Space

Make sure you clear out clutter from your desk before you start work or finish it in the evening. These items include coffee mugs.

pens. hair bands. headphones. books. documents. All of these items should be put away in a neat place. If you know that you will be distracted by the television while working from home and you need to turn it off, then you can switch off your TV.

You may be less productive at work if your workspace is cluttered. This can lead to you procrastinating more and focusing more on your possessions and distracting yourself from work. This can make you feel frustrated and stressed. It is possible to make your workspace cleaner and get rid of distractions that could distract you from your work. This will help you be more productive and organize your day better.

Learn to Let go

It can be hard for people to let go old memories and emotional attachments. Some people are able to quickly forget about an incident and move on, while others carry them around for years or even decades before they are ready to let go. There could be a reason you are holding onto a memory of an individual or event. Or, it might be that something in your house reminds you of them. It is not easy to let go. But it is essential that we do so, in order to heal and move on.

Slow Down

It is a good idea to take a walk, or go outside if you feel overwhelmed. Doing this will allow you to slow down and focus on the things you need and the steps to reach them. You can do this while you are away from your workplace or outside. Take a deep breathe in and hold it. Next, let it out slowly. Continue this process until you are calm.

Once you are calmed down take in what's happening around and you. It has been my experience that if you force yourself to think of other things than the task at hand, it makes me less focused. For instance, I think about what I am making for dinner and the plans for the weekend. When my mind has looked at other options, I'm able to refocus and understand the task better.

Limit Your Social Media Usage

You can limit your social media usage to reduce the noise and thoughts that pervade your brain. Information is constantly being absorbed from various sources, such as Facebook, Twitter or news websites. Our brains can only absorb so much information before we get overwhelmed. Before you know it you are focusing on the headlines and celebrities instead of what you should focus on.

The information will continue to circulate throughout our minds as we work. This can cause us to become more distracted and less productive. You should limit the amount of social media you use throughout the day.

Doing this will reduce your chances of being tempted to purchase something you have seen in a commercial. It will also help us to avoid negative and unhappiness-inducing content. It is also a way to make sure that we don't find unreliable information.

Establish a routine

It's a great way to reduce mental clutter and get more done each day by developing a routine. It can be stressful to have to remember everything all the time, which can make you anxious and less productive. To counter this, it is important to establish a daily routine. This will allow you to not worry so much about what to do next and what you might have forgotten.

You have several options to create a routine. If you use the spreadsheet/document method, you can mark each task and check what is next. The alarm clock method is my preferred method of reminding me. I'm able to plan my days and have my alarms reminding me of any important events throughout the day.

Prioritize Your Tasks

It can be overwhelming to have so many things on your plate. Write down all your tasks and plan your day. This will allow you to concentrate on what's important. A spreadsheet, a notepad or a journal can be used to organize your day. You can also write down the tasks that you need to complete each day, and then assign a time to them.

Doing this will allow you to plan your day easier and decrease the amount of stress you put on yourself to remember each task. This will allow you to be happier, more productive, and help you get through the day. Once you're done with each task, you can mark it off your to-do list and move on.

It is important to only do as much as possible in the day. Don't put pressure on yourself. If you have eight tasks to complete in an hour, you'll be busy for the rest of your day. But if you have 12 tasks to complete and you only have eight hours, one task will take you more than an hour. You might not finish all of your tasks on time. It is important to have realistic goals you are able to achieve.

Prioritizing tasks is key to keeping organized. To manage and prioritize my tasks, I use the 1-2-3 approach. The number one will indicate that the task has to be completed immediately, while two and three are of moderate priority, respectively. The number 1, 2, or 3, depending on how urgent, will be placed next to each task.

You should start your day with the most important tasks. Next, work on your medium priorities. This strategy will help you eliminate the most stressful tasks from the day. This can reduce the stress and mental fatigue that may result from trying to finish urgent tasks before you end work.

Stop Multitasking

National Public Radio's research shows that our brains have never been programmed to concentrate on more than one subject at a given time. (Hamilton and 2008). This is especially true when we have to manage two very important jobs at once.

You can become distracted from one task at the same time and lose your focus, which can lead to slower thinking, drained mental processes, and less productivity. You may also notice silly errors, such as missing a word or attaching an incorrect image to a PowerPoint.

Instead, concentrate on only one task at the time. This will allow you to be less stressed and more precise with your work. It also allows you to work more efficiently and effectively with your time. This will allow you to slow down so that your day is not overwhelming.

To plan your day's tasks, you can use my 1-2-3 method for prioritizing. You should tackle each task individually, in the order they are most important. Once your day is completed, you will find that you feel less stressed and not as exhausted than if you had been multitasking.

Meditation and Yoga

Meditation and yoga are great activities that can help you declutter and relax your mind from the stress and emotions you feel throughout the day. Begin meditation by sitting down with your legs crossed. Your hands should be on your legs. Close your eyes. Once you feel relaxed, focus your attention on your breathing. Take a deep inhale and let it fill you. Next, take a slow exhale. Allow your mind to wander, and then let it go. Your thoughts do not need to be specific. Instead, you can follow the flow of your thoughts.

While you are sitting, you need to be present and aware of the thoughts and emotions you are feeling. After you are ready to move, open your eyes. This will allow you to become more attuned to the world around you and to the smells and sounds you are hearing. During this time, take a seat and note how you are physically, mentally, and emotionally.

After your meditation session, you should feel calmer. You will feel less anxious and stressed. Meditation does not have to take too long. You can start with a minute per day, then work your way up to 10 or 15 minutes. It is important to stay in a state of meditation for as long and as you can. If you are still feeling tense after 15 minutes of meditation, you can then sit longer until your body starts to relax.

Yoga is another great way to declutter and relax after a long day. After a long work day, I love to watch a yoga DVD and listen to the instructor. You can also play some calm music, or turn off the TV if the instructor is talking, while you are practicing yoga. This will allow you to fully immerse in what you are doing. You can also use a guide yoga book for this activity. Yoga relieves tension from the body and allows you to relax after a hectic day.

You can then go about your evening as normal after you've completed yoga. You'll notice a difference in your energy and feeling lighter.

Chapter 12: How You Can Overcome Your Digital Addiction

Addiction can be a form of mental slavery. An addict takes away your free will. You are deprived of your willpower, which can lead to a feeling of overwhelm and de-energized.

Addiction is, however, largely self-inflicted, unlike other forms of slavery. As such, most addicts are voluntarily committing it. Many are now suffering from digital addiction. It negatively impacts people's mental and physical health as well as causing them to lose their productive lives.

It is important to look at addiction as a phenomenon so that we can better understand the causes of digital addiction.

What is Addiction and How Does It Work?

Addiction is the condition in which a person takes part in an act or consumes a substance to obtain rewarding effects. This incentive can make it a compelling motivation for a recurrent pursuit, despite the negative consequences.

What Causes Addiction in People

Many factors can lead to addiction. Each person is different. There are deeper roots than symptoms and consequences. They aren't visible or easy to see. But, cutting off the branches to prevent the growth of flowers and fruit will not solve the addiction.

Addictions' Root Causes

There are three major root causes of addiction. These three main roots are what lead to secondary and third-degree addictions.

* Mental hook

* Adaptation

* Higher experience

Mental Hook

Mental hook refers the factors of the brain that draw people towards digital addiction. These elements act as a magnet to digital technology. Altering brain chemical can lead to a mental hook. Alteration in brain chemistry can be caused by two things:

* Pre-abuse of mental alteration

* Post-abuse mental alternate

Before digital abuse, pre-abuse psychological alteration is common. It can often be caused by mental illness or depression.

Post-abuse mental alteration occurs after digital abuse. It is caused by digital abuse which leads to a vicious triggering of more digital technology abuse. This is secondary.

Digital abuse is the misuse or misapplication of digital technology.

Adaptation

Digital technology can be used as a coping tool to adapt. It could also be because you are trying to deal with:

* Extreme pain - This can be physical, psychological, or emotionally. This is common with social networks. Some people turn to social media for help with psychological or emotional trauma. This could be separation, spousal abuse and divorce. So social media is a place where people can vent their frustrations, or get support.

* Phobia – Phobias can be described as unfounded fears. FOMO (Fear or Missing Out), is the most common phobia that encourages people to abuse technology. Some people fear missing the news, special offers and breaking news.

* Environmental constraints - coping with a hostile environment like quarantine (such COVID-19), isolation or being in a refugee tent, harsh weather and others can lead to some people developing digital addiction.

* Peer pressure – Teenagers are at greatest risk of peer pressure. Teens are often pressured to copy others to feel like they are part of the group. Peer pressure can also be a

problem for grownups, but they are not as vulnerable to it as teenagers. Teenagers often join social media networks due to peer pressure. Snapchat and Instagram are the most popular social media networks that teens join due to peer pressure.

Higher Experience

One can desire to have an amazing experience so they may try digital technology tools. They will continue to use it to maintain that experience.

The Higher Experience

* Enhanced performance - the desire and ability to perform well in exams or athletic contests. In order to increase their sexual prowess, pornography may be an option.

* Ecstasy: The desire to feel good. This could make it easier to invest in the latest technology, enjoy VR more, and even try digital sex toys.

Key Elements of Addiction

These are the essential elements of addiction.

* Reward is a gain that is perceived or actual.

* Motivation (trigger): There is a strong incentive to pursue the reward.

* Reinforcement (routine - This is a repeatable action that reinforces the habit.

* Memory - The reward from the past acts to encourage repetition.

* Impaired Control - Each reinforcement wears down one's willpower.

* Compulsion — When you have impaired control, it becomes almost effortless to fall into an addiction.

* Negative outcomes - The addiction can have serious mental, psychological, emotional and/or financial consequences.

It's easy to see that the first four elements (reward, motivation, reinforcement, reinforcement, memory) are closely connected to habit formation.

* The reward is exactly the same element that was in the habit formation

* Reinforcement can be used in place of routine in habit formation

* Motivation is the same thing as a trigger in habit formation.

* Memory can be used in habit formation as the same way as a cue. A trigger activates when it is given a signal called a cue.

These two factors are related. The impaired control, compulsion, as well as the adverse consequences, are often more severe for addiction.

Types Of Addiction

Knowing about addiction types will help you recognize the type of addiction your loved one is suffering from and how to handle it. Some addictions can be so obvious that it is easy to spot when someone you love is addicted. But there are many other addictions, and if you don't know, you might not recognize them. It's difficult to recognize someone else as addicted, particularly teenagers. Teenagers can present a problem for caregivers and parents as they engage in secretive addictive behaviors that are not subject to any restrictions. They are able to skirt rules in a horrible way.

There are many types addictions. But they can be broken down into two broad categories.

* Substance abuse

* Behavioral addiction

Substance Addiction

Substance addiction, which is a progressive relapsing illness that can result from compulsive substance misuse, is not something one should be aware of. This condition can make it difficult to quit or control the substance.

Digital addiction is a behavioral problem, but it is not unusual to find people who abuse digital technology while also abusing substance. While there may not be a direct causal relationship between substance or behavioral abuse, it is not unusual for them to act in complementarity. For instance, people who use digital gadgets to get sexual pleasure are more likely be involved in substance abuse before or during the act.

Two key factors allow for substance addiction:

* Tolerance

* Dependence

Tolerance means that the body is able to tolerate a certain amount of the same chemical substance. Users will have to consume greater quantities of the same product in order achieve the same level.

Dependence refers to the need to consume certain substances in order to feel normal. Withdrawal symptoms occur when the user is unable to consume the substance in sufficient quantities or fails to take the prescribed dosage. This makes them feel "abnormal." To return to normalcy, the user will need to consume the substance in greater quantities than the tolerance.

Addictive Substances

There are many kinds of addictive substances. These addictive substances can be divided into five main categories.

* Stimulants

* Hallucinogens

* Depressants

* Opioids

* Dissociatives

The most frequently abused substance by digital addicts is stimulants. Many people spend long hours online and consume a lot coffee in an attempt to stay awake, alert, and less tired.

Behavioral Addictions

Behavioral addiction can be defined as a compulsive, uncontrollable desire to engage in rewarding, non-drug-related activities even if it has negative consequences for the person's emotional, physical, social and/or economic well being. Digital addiction is a type of behavioral addiction.

The following are common signs of behavioral addiction:

* An obsession with addictive behavior that is consistent

* Inability to control addictive behavior

* Greater tolerance to addictive behavior

* Being dependent on addictive behavior to cope with emotional disturbances

* Sacrificing other productive activities, such as family, education, work, and so on. Behavioral addiction

* Reducing or concealing the severity of your addiction

* Adverse withdrawal symptoms if you resist or avoid the behavior

* Psychological withdrawal signs such as anxiety or depressive symptoms when you resist the behavior or try to avoid it.

Exercises that indicate a severe case of behavioral addiction

* Doing or speaking harmful things as a result.

* Harming loved people because of the addictive behavior

* Losing your valuables or compromising your relationship because of addictive behavior

These are all behavioral addictions that may be compounded with digital addiction.

* Recreational addiction

* Relationship addiction

* Shopping addiction

* Work addiction

Digital Addiction

It is obvious that we live in a digitalized world. It is difficult to imagine living without computers. Each day we use a digital device in some way.

Some digital systems have even made us addicted. Do you feel angry, frustrated, moody or irritated every time you lose power? If you do, then you either have a digital addiction or are slowly falling into digital addiction.

The following are the most common types of digital dependence:

* Internet addiction

* Social media addiction

* Addiction to videogames

Shopping addiction

If you shop too often, you may become addicted to shopping. You can have shopping addiction in one of two ways:

* Impulsive shopping - where you buy something immediately without planning or thinking.

* Sentimental shopping - This is different from impulse buying. It involves buying sentimentally, which means you make purchases based on emotions. For example, you could buy anniversary gifts (birthdays/weddings/graduation, etc.). A form of sentimental shopping is buying gifts for loved ones. But you do not necessarily have to buy. However, you may be buying because of a nostalgic feeling. The same applies to jewelry, souvenirs, or expensive timepieces.

If there's one product category that can induce shopping addiction, it is the digital category. Think about smartphones. Shopaholics love to shop for the latest and greatest smartphones.

Work addiction

The most common form of work addiction among career workers is called "work addiction". Work addiction is when you don't know the difference between work and personal time so you end up working more than you should. People who stay up late at work are not always in need of work. They do so because it's difficult to get away from their desks. Some can't even make it through the one week holiday without returning to the office.

In the digital age, work addiction has grown more severe. It is possible to work remotely in this digital age. It is simple to work remotely from your home or office while also extending your working hours. It is becoming more difficult to tell the line between working in an office and home. This is due to a pandemic like COVID-19.

It is wonderful to work from anywhere, whether you are at home or in an office. For people who already workaholics, digital technology makes it even worse. Workaholics could be pushed from work by the closing of their offices. This is impossible with digital technology.

Addiction Triggers

Triggers play an important role in reinforcing addictive behavior. Triggers cause cravings, and can even lead to an urge. A trigger is simply a cue to urge a person to take an addictive substance or engage with addictive behavior.

There are two main types.

* Internal triggers

* External triggers

Internal Triggers

These triggers originate in the inside of one's own mind. These triggers could be thoughts, feelings or memories that become sensitized. This can lead to urges, cravings, and other behaviors.

There are three main types internal triggers.

* Emotions

* Physical sensations

* Attitudes

Emotions

Emotions are among the most addictive triggers. Here are some common emotions which can lead to addictive tendencies.

* Phobia

* Anxiety

* A feeling of loneliness

* Self-Pity

* Resentment

* Anger

* Indifference

* Boredom

* Fatigue

* Frustration

* Stress

* Depression

* Other negative feelings one subconsciously strives to avoid

Anxiety and Phobia

Phobia refers to an extreme, irrational fear that can cause severe anxiety or disrupt your ability to function normally.

Phobia has two components.

* Catastrophic thought - Thinking about something that could go wrong

* Evasive Behavior - Preventing the occurrence or reoccurrence of the perceived catastrophe

People suffering from certain phobias are more likely to use marijuana or drink to cope.

Some of the most common phobias linked to addiction are:

* Social phobia (fear and anxiety about public interactions) - This can lead to one seeking substance abuse to make them feel more comfortable in social situations.

* Ochlophobia (fear and fear of crowds), - this can trigger emotional or social triggers.

* Glossophobia (fear and aversion to public speaking): This may lead one to use substance abuse in an attempt to gain public confidence.

* Monophobia (fear and resentment of being alone): This may lead to anger or self-pity, clinging, and obsession.

Some people use social media as a way to express themselves and to avoid having to face their fears. This includes glossophobia, monophobia, ochlophobia and even social phobia. Digital addiction is possible.

Physical Sensations

When physical sensations are connected to something you seek to treat with a drug or other addictive behavior, they can lead to addictive tendencies.

Here are some common sensations of body:

* Pain

* Fatigue

* Panic

* Hunger

* Sexual arousal

* Senses (smells, tastes, sounds, touch, sight, etc.)

Some people visit pornographic sites due to sexual arousal. This can lead to an addiction that could then turn into a digital addiction. Pornography is the main addiction. Digital addiction is a secondary.

External Triggers

External triggers refer to those that occur outside of the body. Here are the top two types:

* Environmental triggers

* Social triggers

Environmental Triggers

The cues that trigger your addiction tendencies are called environmental triggers. The two main types are:

* Places

* All Things

Places

The addictive tendencies can be triggered by a pattern of visiting or being in certain places.

These high-risk locations can cause addictive tendencies.

* Worksites (digital work addiction)

* Shopping malls (shopping addiction)

* Online gambling sites (digital gambling addiction)

* Online dating sites (digital dating addiction)

* Digital pornographic addiction (pornographic sites)

* Cybercafes (digital addiction)

Cybercafes online gambling websites, eCommerce sites, freelancing sites and cybercafes could lead to digital addiction for gamblers, workaholics, and shopaholics.

Things

We often use certain items while we are addicted to substances or engaging in addictive behaviors. These things can trigger addictive tendencies.

These high-risk situations can lead to addictive tendencies.

* Smart cards (debit/credit), - Digital shopping addiction

* Idle digital devices - digital touch addiction

* Game consoles, digital video games addiction

* Headsets for digital music addiction

* Television/movies – (pornography and sex addictions, food addictions, etc.

TVs as well as smartphones, computer monitors, games consoles, headphones, and smartcards can all trigger digital addiction.

Situations

Repetitive tendencies can be more triggered by certain situations or events.

The following situations/events are likely to trigger addictive tendencies.

* Emotionally charged conversations - e.g. angry news, political arguments or criticism

* Holidays/Celebrations/Sporting Events - e.g. anniversaries, graduations.

* Time-based events include: breakfast (coffee), breaks (junkie snack), lunch and dinner (bingeing), weekends, alcohol), Christmas season, Bingeing, Alcoholism), cold-season (coffee).

People can turn to social media and other online forums to vent their anger and to hear from others. Because news and politics do not take a vacation, it can become a habitual and lead to digital addiction. People who use digital devices to entertain themselves and for leisure may find it more difficult to enjoy holidays and weekends with them. If you are one among those photographers who cannot stop using digital cameras, holidays may be the perfect time to indulge your digital addiction (camera addiction).

How to Deal with Digital Addiction

Addiction can lead to serious consequences. Some of these consequences are reverseable, others irreversible, and some can even be fatal. It is important that you are aware of the effects of addiction and can take steps to manage them. There is a higher risk of failing to recognize the damage already done and relapsing once recovery has been completed.

It is not just one's addiction that affects you, but also your loved ones, family members, and colleagues.

Digital addiction can have many negative consequences, including:

* A loss of productivity

* Wastefulness: Wasting time and money

* Any illness that is associated with a sedentary lifestyle, such as diabetes, obesity, or other conditions.

* Loss or fragmentation of productive social relations

* Lost labor hours – Employees'moonlighting' over their smartphones and computers may result in employers losing many hours of labor that they paid for. This is a huge drain on their profits

Preventing a Relapse

Recovering from digital addiction is a huge leap. However, recovery is not a guarantee of no regression. It is important to avoid relapses in order to create a barrier that prevents you from sliding back.

As your resolve weakens and your willpower wears out, every time you relapse, it is harder to stay strong. Relapse prevention is crucial, no matter what cost.

To avoid relapse, you must first learn about its common causes.

Chapter 13: Making Minimalistic Decisions And The Benefits It Offer

Being able to access almost all of the things we need means that we are surrounded by abundance.

There are many great things about living a life of abundance. But, there are also some downsides.

Too Many Choices are a Bad Thing

Too many options create pressure to make a final decision.

Are you aware of how difficult it can become to make a choice when you are tired. Even the simplest task can become overwhelming when you are low on energy.

This is because making a decision with so many choices can be overwhelming.

Two types of thinking exist when it comes time to make decisions. The first is pre-programmed and relies heavily on instinctual and receptive decisions. The second stage allows for contemplation. This mode is responsible to making critical decisions based logic and facts.

First, let me talk about the second. We can only make sensible decisions using the second mode of decision making when our mental tank is full.

Google's thorough search results revealed that humans can make around 35,000 decisions daily. This category also includes impulse-based decisions. This category includes both expository as well as instinctual decisions. Our main objective in minimalism, however, is to include only the second type of decision.

Scientists believe that our brains regularly make 75 conscious choices. The differences between this and 35,000 are obvious, but the mind remains stubborn.

These seventy-five options require a clear head as well as a sharp mind. There are many options and each one has its own benefits and drawbacks.

To make up for this, we make this decision 75 times daily. We are responsible for making decisions like whether we bring umbrellas to the beach, whether we hike or use UBER, what pizza or sushi to order, whether we take a stroll or watch a flick, or whether to watch video games or watch movies. It is not difficult to see how many decisions we need to make each day. You can see why we get exhausted before the end of every day!

Because your decision-making capacity is limited to 75 decisions, it's a good idea to start with the most crucial ones and work your ways down to the less important. This will allow you to get rid of a lot more clutter in your daily life.

Daily micro-decisions (such as choosing shoes or reacting to a multipurpose action) seem to sap energy that is needed to settle on the major ones. It is important to keep to the most important decisions only at all times.

What happens if you don't have any other options? It is as easy to make fewer impulsive choices and devote less time to secondary considerations. It would mean that you could still focus on more urgent matters.

Here's where the idea of minimalism comes in.

Minimalism is good for preserving vitality, and it helps with stress relief.

While it might not seem obvious, minimalism is a way to save energy.

Good judgment is essential if you want to feel happy. For us to make well-informed decisions, we must have mental vigour. It is important to not waste this vitality.

You may make healthier decisions at any hour of your day or night. Before this point it would have been impossible to exercise or to write experimentally after a long working day. These types of decisions are now complicated by inconsequential paperwork.

Stopping mental energy wasting is as simple as getting rid of all unnecessary items. We need to be minimalists as it stands.

After removing the extraneous, we will live a life that is free of excess. Despite the fact that there are less options, all choices you make will be good.

Saying "no" when you have the opportunity, "you're beginning to eliminate compulsiveness," states the author. The act of not cutting hairs reduces emotional heaviness.

Minimalism will make you feel lighter, from the inside. A minimalist lifestyle is the best way to have better decisions and more energy.

Minimalist living can be achieved with minimal effort.

Minimalism is an excellent option for those who want to live a more happy, stress-free and vibrant life. It is up you to decide if it is worth your time.

It is not necessary that you become an extreme minimalist, limiting your possessions to 25. This approach is not right for everyone. You can start small and gradually increase your efforts.

Consider the areas that would be the most benefit from a minimalist approach to your life. Make a list and then start implementing the methods. What are your options to create a simple strategy?

Consider these:

Consider how you can improve your dining experience the next time that you visit a restaurant. Instead of looking at every item on the list to determine the best option, order the first thing that you notice. You have the option to eat lunch at a different place each weekday. Alternately, you may wear the exact same pair of shoes to work each morning. The best strategy is to start small, and slowly add more strategies. It's more about making things simpler for everyone.

The long-term benefits of a minimalist lifestyle are the same regardless of the reason. Better judgment, better mental stamina, and overall better quality of your life are all benefits. It doesn't matter why.

You will notice the big changes in your lives eventually, and you won't regret it.

It is obvious it will be difficult. The beginning of any project is the most difficult. The first step did not have much to do with the final task. It is necessary to make a choice before you can begin. To make a decision. Let me tell you, the decision that you make will have a profound impact on your entire life.

The hardest task is taking action to change. It is, in reality, the polar opposite to procrastination. This is something you and me both know is easy. As simple as this may sound, there is no real benefit.

Implementing long-term change can be very difficult. This is why it is so important to choose to take initiative and to actually do something.

Two types of decisions are important to think about: the emotional and intellectual.

You are able to see that there is a need for change in your life. You realize that you are unfulfilled, unhappy and worried. You realize that freedom is not something you have. Whatever the case, the problem is you don't understand the facts and aren't aware of them. It's unlikely you will be willing to accept that things have to change. They need to change. But you aren't sure why.

Should vs. Required

It works the same way with everything you say to yourself.

You must stop wasting your money.

You should see fewer TV shows and movies.

Get rid everything from your closet.

Your behaviour should be changed.

More nutritious foods are needed.

You should exercise.

It's a good idea for employees to work shorter hours.

You should read more.

It is all about the ifs, ifs, and ifs, ifs, ifs, ifs, ifs, ifs, ifs, ifs, fifs, ifs, ifs, ifs?

After you have procrastinated for so long, you eventually feel like poo.

If you believe in the importance and passion of advancement, you can transform your shoulds into musts. It is important to first compare the suffering and our current circumstances. Then, compare the pleasure of the new outcome. You can make your should(s), a must, by creating a balance of pain and pleasure.

This is where the process begins.

You have to act in this circumstance.

The shift becomes second nature and eventually you will make a choice.

You can't make a romantic decision until it becomes a need. When your must(s), at exactly, has turned into a need, can you say you have made an honest decision. This would be the following:

Modifications are required.

You should work less.

You should eat more healthy foods.

Stop wasting money.

You must exercise.

You should get rid off all your junk.

It is now a matter if you must have consistent musts.

Your Must List is all you need right now. What are you most passionate about? What will bring extreme joy or anguish to you? Spend some time writing down your must-dos.

These musts need to be declared loudly for everyone to hear. Are the musts convincing you more than your current should(s), or are they? The Should List, which is powerless, slow, and dormant is far more convincing than the Must List, which is determined, impassioned. While the first day doesn't involve moving (we will move every other day), the first step is still the most difficult. You have to take the first step in changing things now. You know, at least mentally, that you don't like the way things are in large parts of your daily life. It's impossible to have it everywhere. However, it's not possible to expect it to be that way if your actions and thoughts show otherwise. If your actions and thoughts are not in harmony with your desires, you will never be content, happy, satisfied, or satisfied.

Re-evaluate your Must-Have List. Post it where you see it frequently. This will enable you to make an informed decision. One that will have a significant impact in your life. It will inspire you to live the life you desire. Feel the change in your stomach and body.

Make today the most important moment in your entire life. Because your life is about changing dramatically, today is the day you must make your should(s). You've made the decision to act today. Today is the beginning of your new, normal, and untangled existence.

Chapter 14: How To Make Digital Minimalism Your Way In Life

Digital minimalism should be considered a lifestyle. Digital minimalism should be considered a lifestyle, not a temporary option. We have so far viewed it in this manner. We are trying to find the root cause of digital addiction, digital abuse and digital consumerism. Not just to treat the symptoms.

Make digital minimalism your life style

Plan Your Time

Digital minimalism relies on time management. It is this false sense that we have "plenty" of free time that causes many to "waste" time on social networks and other online platforms.

But this false notion of "free", or "free," time is often due to the lack of a time-table and assigned tasks. Many people discover later that they have "forgotten" to do certain important tasks. These non-performances accumulate over time and have a negative impact on your health, earnings, and skills. It can also lead to lower productivity and interpersonal tensions. These areas are often neglected when you spend your "free" online time. And the consequences of this can come back to haunt you later.

To plan your time properly:

* Use a complex time-table (a school time-table is an example)

* Schedule your tasks

* Create a To Do List and make sure to keep it up-to-date

* Gantt Charts are a great way to manage your projects. Get into the habit for batching tasks and creating projects.

* Apply the Critical Path Method to prioritize tasks within your project.

You can also use electronic tools. However, digital tools can be used to great effect. It is best to stick to pen and paper, rather than using digital gadgets. It is a great way to strengthen your ideas and keep them in your memory.

Budget for Your Purchases

Yes, impulse buying fuels digital consumerism. Impulse purchasing is a behavior that results from having "free" money but not being allocated to a meaningful project. There is no compelling reason to use your cash for this project, and you lack the motivation to stick with it. Therefore, you often buy things impulsively because they appear to have the tendency to draw your attention to quick, but fleeting inspiration.

So that your emotions are connected to the project, create it. This will make you more aware of your emotions and reduce impulse-buying.

Make sure you have short-term, long-term, and medium-term goals. So, short-term initiatives can be absorbed by medium-term and long-term projects.

When you have completed inspiring projects, be sure to give them enough money. Pay attention to them. Give them sufficient attention. If they are motivational enough, you won't have to be so hard on yourself to pay attention and focus on them.

To ensure that you have more cash on hand, you can buy your daily consumables far in advance. Non-perishables can be stored on a weekly or two-weekly basis. Perishables are best kept in the fridge for at least two days. The less you go to shopping malls, and the less likely that you will impulse buy digital gadgets,

Completely avoid credit cards. Instead, use a Prepaid credit card. Avoid online and mobile money transfers to avoid being tempted to visit mobile or online platforms.

You should consider the opportunity cost of using digital technology

As we've seen, it is not enough to just consider the price for a digital gadget/technology. Price is only one cost. There is much more to cost than price.

The real cost is what it costs to get the next best opportunity. This opportunity is not only monetary. It's also about time, skill, productivity and job promotion.

You should consider the opportunity cost if you overindulge in social media. If you decide to own three or more smartphones, think about the opportunity costs. Consider the opportunity price if you opt to stay inside for long periods of time while watching TV or playing video games on the couch.

When evaluating the cost-benefit ratio of the purchase of a certain digital gadget/technology, you should consider the opportunity costs.

Discover the Best Alternatives to Digital Consumption

In digital minimalism, substitution can be the best policy. Digital minimalism does NOT mean that you have to forgo the many benefits of digital technology. This is more about enjoying these benefits at the lowest cost.

It is possible to enjoy the same benefits from non-digital consumption but with a more affordable price. So why not try that alternative? This affordability should be evaluated not only in terms if the price but also in terms opportunites cost.

If you have a limited list of groceries to remember while shopping, write it on a piece or paper. It is cheaper and much more convenient.

Other non-digital options may be available that accomplish the same purpose, but at a lower chance cost.

Your Digital Space should be constantly decluttered

As we know, the digital area is vast. This includes places to keep your digital devices - such as the house table, office table, car's dashboard and pockets, handbags, etc. It also includes your data and apps, such as screen, storage memory, and screen.

Digital clutter can be reduced to make your space more efficient. Digital clutter will not only take up space but can also distract from your attention. Digital clutter can not only distract but also create a bad habit: you will find yourself constantly fidgeting on your digital devices or scanning the web for the latest information.

Prioritize Your Choices

We have seen the value of cost-benefit analysis. You can't use these tools or techniques unless and until you know what your priorities are.

When it comes to your choices, planning is the most important thing. Plan first, but don't forget to cultivate a planning mindset. A planning mindset will make prioritizing a breeze and less tedious than it used to be.

Develop a planning mindset that is your most important, first and foremost priority. It will make it easy to plan, create a budget, and present your plans. Digital minimalism is not something that should be forced on you.

Chapter 15: How Do You Organize Your Bathroom?

Your bathroom sink is the first thing you should clear out when decluttering. It is best to completely remove it, then clean it up until it is spotless and fully disinfected. Do not return any of the contents. Make sure to empty and clean out your medicine cabinets. This is where we want to make sure that as little material as possible remains on the surface surrounding the sink. Decluttering and organizing your medicine cabinet before replacing any items will allow you to have additional storage space. It is worth considering storing items in other places in your bathroom if they aren't being used regularly.

It is easy to forget the expiration dates for prescription and over-the-counter medicines, cosmetics and personal care items. Verify the expiration dates. Don't throw away expired medicine. Don't toss out expired medicines in the trash. To find out the best way to dispose of expired medicine in your area, go online.

Most cosmetics and personal care products don't have expiration days. But, that doesn't necessarily mean they never expire. Is it possible to smell them fresh or do they have a rotten aroma? What has happened to the texture or color of the item? Do not hesitate to throw it out if in doubt. This is especially important for items close to your eyes.

Once you've decluttered your medicine cabinet, take out what you think will be useful. Then you can put away the items that are no longer needed. Limit this to hand soap and hand lotion, as well as toothbrushes. Consider placing extra items on the sink in a container or tray that can be waterproofed.

Move on to the toilet. Get rid of anything that is still on the surface. Make sure to thoroughly clean and disinfect your toilet. You should also remember to disinfect items such as toilet brushes.

Next, we need to address the larger storage space in your bathroom. You probably have cleaning products underneath the sink. Are they still good quality? Do you use them in the toilet? If so, they should either be removed or moved. It is important to properly separate items stored next to cleaning products. You don't want the tip of your toilet bowl cleaner touching anything on your body.

If you have accumulated a lot cosmetic samples and personal care products. It is easy to save these items for trips or "someday." Be honest with your self. How often do your trips take you? Do you make the effort to organize and pack your sample collection before you go on vacation? If you have them saved for "someday", they probably won't get used. Donate these items at your homeless shelter. If you have any spare items, it will be a great help to someone who is in dire need.

Do people give you bath gels or scented lotions as gifts? Are there more things than you use each year? Add these items to your donation pile. Are you a man who keeps a lot of disposable razors and hasn't shaved in years to grow a mustache? Donate those razors.

Do you have hair dryers that are more useful than the people who live in your house? Donate your extras. In this situation, I recommend that you keep one spare. They often break suddenly. Do you still have the eighties crimper in your life? You should throw it out.

Once you have cleared your space, it's time to get rid of the clutter. It may be a good idea to have one bin per person for the bathroom that contains all your items. This might be a good choice if you have a toddler or teenager and two parents sharing the bathroom. Different sizes of bins are not necessary. The size of the bin should be indicative of how big you want your stash to be. It's a good idea if you don't share a bathroom to store items that are similar. Label the bins with things such as "bath, body", "bath toys," teeth, "teeth" and "first aid." Your bath gels or lotions are already full so you won't have to buy any more. You might be amazed at the amount of items in your storage that you discover as you organize. Declutter some more!

The best place to store your most important items is the same as in other rooms. Only exception is your first aid kit.

While you may not need to reach them often, they should always be readily accessible. Your beach towels could be stored in your bathroom in winter. You can place them on top shelves that are difficult to reach without a stepladder. Separate towels for pets that bathe in the bathroom. To make it easy for family members to identify the dog towels, cut off one corner.

It's now time for you to use the bathtub and shower. Remove everything. Wash the shower curtains if they are needed. If it is necessary, wash or replace the shower curtain liner. You should scrub the shower and bathtub, along with any containers, racks, or storage areas. Only replace any items that are frequently used. All the rest can go in your bins. Finally, mop your floors.

After you're done, enjoy a refreshing bubble bath! Undoubtedly, there are few things that can be as relaxing as a hot bath in a freshly cleaned bathroom.

Do the same thing for all half and full baths in your home.

Tips for maintaining your bathroom

* Wash the sink at least once a day. You can get rid of clutter that has built up there. Take a few moments each day to clean out clutter. You will reduce the amount of deep cleaning you have to do every week.

* Every day, flush a toilet bowl with a brush. You will find your toilet is easier to clean and won't take as long.

* Don't overfill your bins. Check your bins before you go shopping. You might already have a backup for the item that you were looking for. Declutter the bins again if they get full.

* Avoid opening too many items at once. How many bath gels will you use in the rotation? Do not keep more than the minimum in your shower. Rest of the items can go in your bin. You can keep the items for longer if you don't open them. To note the date on a new purchase or opening, you can use waterproof markers. This will remind to throw it out when it's old and will also give you an idea how long it takes for you to use different items.

* The bathroom can be a place where you can relax and treat yourself. A "Me Time" container can be used to store bubble bath, great-smelling candles, your favorite bodywash, and luxurious lotion.

* Apply a daily shower gel after each bath. This will reduce build-up and make it easier to clean the shower. These products work best when used in a clean bath or tub. They are more preventative then proactive.

Hyper Hummingbirds might consider setting a timer that runs for five minutes per day so they can deep clean their homes instead of trying to do everything at once. Do the washing up one day, then the washing up the next. Make sure you check your supplies and finish the task before the timer goes off. Make sure you have everything organized and make a list.

* While busy Beavers need to maintain the kitchen, they may prefer to choose one day for deep cleaning.

* Goal for its Grophers may try to set challenges such as how deep they can clean while their child is in a bath. This works well for young children that need supervision but can clean their own baths.

* Do not allow magazines to collect in the bathroom. You can only imagine how many unwashed hands are handling the

same item over and over again. You can't sanitize a magazine.

Chapter 16: Applying Minimalism To Meditation

It is important to remember that the ultimate objective of this moderation endeavor is to create a genuine sense and joy. This is why we'll be discussing reflection. Reflection holds the key to your deepest harmony, and will show you the way towards genuine satisfaction and lasting joy.

What struck a chord with people who talk about contemplation in their conversations? What is it about Eastern examples that involve dark and desolate methods of supplication? That could be frightening and exhausting. We are not talking about that kind of meditation.

Meditation is a way to get rid of all the noise and focus on your inner peace. It's a journey to self-disclosure. It's amazing to see how individuals cross countries and landmass trying to find themselves. It's a similar self that they should find and communicate with.

We look to the outside for a sense of peace and joy that lasts. It is the common way of life, but moderation looks within you and around to see all you are looking for. You don't need to look for fulfillment outside of things. The moderation and restrained display of contemplation will lead you to the genuine fulfillment only found inside.

Meditation requires you to focus more attention on one or two articles. The most important and powerful reflection is to zero in on the breath. While we are fully aware of how much air we breathe, we are far too preoccupied to let go of the relaxation cycle. To be able see the seemingly insignificant details that really matter around you, to distract from the astounding interruptions in society.

Without being retargeted, it's impossible to search the web for anything again. Everywhere you look, there are ads. With each one of these, we find it more difficult to stay focused on the important things.

Our lives really do matter. What reflection does is help us put our focus back on what really matters.

The dynamic care of increased spotlighting your breath, without considering anything else, is what you're doing. It helps you remove interruptions from your brain. It might be difficult to begin with, but it will get easier over time. Your ability to concentrate will improve. By doing this, you can focus your attention on the most important parts of your life.

There are different types of reflection than the standard final product. The benevolent that we are concerned about in moderation is just the simple demonstration of how you can prepare your brain to excessively become used dynamically care so you can control your thoughts.

Mindful Strategies

These techniques can help you achieve the necessary condition of care, also known reflection.

* Start small. The act of caring can seem disappointing at first. To be an ideal person for the underlying circumstances, you should accept the role of a fledgling. It is not necessary to be a master in your first attempt at thinking. It's possible to get lost if you try. It is okay to take your time, take slow, consistent, gradual steps, and you'll get there.

Choose a Meditation-accommodating Environment: in case you *

Do not live alone. Allow others to enter your home. All clutter should be removed from your space. Your brain records what it sees. On the off chance that it detects a mess in your present situation, it will add complexity. That is not good for contemplation. Reflection can be tied to getting your thoughts sorted to narrow in on one idea. Your mind should be ready for it.

* Focus on Only One Thing. We have been focusing our attention on the one thing that matters most.

You can either focus on your own body or a single object, such as a candle. Once you have decided to focus on your breathing, you can then shut your eyes as needed. Then you can observe how you breathe in and exhale out. It's amazing to see how breathing is the core of our existence. Yet, we get so busy that we forget to pay attention. If we stop breathing, then we are gone. It is only a joy to stop and think about our breath. It takes about 20,000 for a person to relax. In meditation, you might be able to see a few of them briefly.

* Reflect on the Fact of Mortality. When someone close to you passes away, we become calm for that instant and the way that it might be us gazes directly into our eyes. Within a matter of days, or even weeks, we'll be extremely aware how we behave, what we say, and with whom we spend our time. Because we have been made to realize our mortality by the passing a beloved one, we will most likely be more aware of how our lives continue.

But, the calm reflection is not something that lasts for very long. Within a few weeks, the individual has been covered and we are back to our normal exercises at full speed. We may in all cases be grieving, tormented, or miss them. However, we will live our normal lives as before the news of their death.

What if we were constantly reminded that we are susceptible to death and it can happen to anyone? What if we realized that the meal we are currently eating could be our last one? What if it is possible to not deny that the extra clothes and cars you are purchasing may never come in handy? What will this do to our thinking and ourselves? It will be a good moment. We won't buy anything we don't need as we know it will be of no use. We will be more open to spending time with our families because we know it may be the last. We will donate money to charity because it is our desire to make a difference in the lives of as many people as possible before we pass on.

This is the reason we must reflect on our mortality. This awareness will help us coordinate our reasoning and focus our attention on the most important things in our lives.

The reality of our mortality doesn't mean we have to dwell on it constantly. That could lead us to negative reasoning or even fear about the day when we are going to die. Everything revolves around the possibility that we will not be ignorant of this possibility. Everything revolves around us realizing that there isn't much between us and someone who has just kicked it and that death is possible.

To reflect on our mortality, you can take a few minutes out of your day to go to a quiet place. This will allow you to place your entire life in perspective. It will be trivial for you to worry about what other people are doing.

Ryan Holiday summarizes it briefly:

We can view time as a gift if we remind ourselves daily that we will soon pass on.

An individual on a cutoff does not entertain himself with unimaginable endeavors. He doesn't just sit there wailing about how things should be. They figure out what they have to do and complete it in the time allowed. They determine how they will survive the second strike.

It is possible to make this update in tranquil meditation.

Reducing Negative Thinking

Normal people have around 50 000 thoughts per day. A majority of them are negative. Negative reasoning is like bile. It ruins the entire system. Stress affects your life. In the case of a marriage, your partner and children are also affected. Already before your kids go to high school you worry about how they will manage college expenses.

Even if you don't have personal stress issues, which can be difficult, there is enough misfortune to keep you up at night. Newsworthy is the constant revelation of individuals who have taken their own lives. The latest news about abuse at home, psychological warfare, and war is constantly being reported.

There is war everywhere.

For you to not get engrossed in negative thinking with any of these, you must do some cognizant work. This will help to divert your attention from the usual idea designs. Find the positives in these negatives so that you can be more optimistic about your own lives. To reduce the negative thought pattern, that is what we mean.

When you practice contemplation you will find that the time you spend dwelling on negative considerations is better spent focusing on your inner identity. This will help you become more prepared to make positive changes in life.

Conclusion

It was a pleasure to read this book. I hope it will help guide you towards decluttering your life, and living a happier and more fulfilled life. It is possible to have many possessions. But, if we give too much value to our possessions, we will be prone to anxiety, stress, or even death.

Technology and its development have led to an increase in clutter and physical, mental, as well as digital clutter in our homes and personal lives. We are constantly being drawn to the temptation of purchasing things - both the ones and ones we do not need.

This lifestyle won't solve our problems, but it can make us feel unsatisfied or anxious. Minimalism, as we've seen above, is the best treatment for these issues.

The information you currently have in your hands to help you defeat "The More

Virus," which allows you to desire more - more cars and more clothes, as well as more alcohol, food, and more appliances.

The more virus can make you unhappy so it is important that you get rid of it. Go ahead, decluttering your life is easy with the steps you've read in this book. A minimalist home will allow you to have a calm and clutter-free existence. Living intentionally is a way to live a more intentional life. Keep your home clutter-free and embrace the things you love.

Apply a minimalist lifestyle to your home and other areas of your life. Socrates' words:

"The secret of happiness, as you can see, is not finding more, but developing the capacity for enjoying less.

www.ingramcontent.com/pod-product-compliance
Lightning Source LLC
Chambersburg PA
CBHW050406120526
44590CB00015B/1849